Jams, Preserves
& Edible Gifts

Cookery books published by the National Trust

National Trust Recipes by Sarah Edington

Healthy Eating by Sarah Edington

Teatime Recipes by Jane Pettigrew

Recipes from the Dairy by Robin Weir and Caroline Liddell with Peter Brears

The Art of Dining by Sara Paston-Williams

A Book of Historical Recipes by Sara Paston-Williams

Jams, Preserves & Edible Gifts

Sara Paston-Williams

Special Photography by Andreas von Einsiedel

The National Trust

First published in Great Britain in 1985 by David & Charles under the title
The Country House Kitchen Store Cupboard

Completely new and revised edition published in Great Britain in 1999 by
National Trust Enterprises Limited, 36 Queen Anne's Gate,
London SW1H 9AS

http://www.ukindex.co.uk/nationaltrust/bookshelf

British Library Cataloguing in Publication Data
A catalogue record for this book is available from the British Library

ISBN 0-7078-0274-1

Designed by the Newton Engert Partnership

Phototypset in Briem Script, Frutiger and Palatino

Printed and bound in Great Britain by Butler & Tanner Ltd, Frome

Contents

To the National Trust's cooks and chefs

Introduction

There are few things more satisfying than opening your store cupboard to reveal jars of glistening jams and jellies, and pots, bottles and boxes full of interesting foods. Whether you are an experienced cook, or rarely approach the stove, making preserves and edible gifts is not difficult and the results are so much better than anything you can buy.

Country housewives have been preserving foods in much the same way for centuries. In the days before refrigerators and freezers, fruit was preserved in honey and sugar, or spiced in vinegar; soft fruits were candied, jellied or made into jam, sauces or syrups. Many vegetables were put into pickles and chutneys. Nuts were stored in wet salt or buried in dry earth, while eggs were pickled or waxed and buried in sawdust. Scents, flavourings and essences from fruit, nuts and flowers were distilled and sealed in flasks. Vegetables, flowers, fruits and herbs produced a variety of wines and drinks.

The great country houses had a special 'still-room'. Originally this was where the lady of the house supervised distilling for medicines and perfumes, and where the preserves and sweetmeats were prepared for the banquet or final course of the dinner. The seventeenth-century 'still-house' at Ham House near Richmond in Surrey survives, with its special stoves for distilling, and the National Trust hope to restore it once the funds can be found.

The laboratory character of these early still-rooms gave way to a more conventional kitchen style in the eighteenth century, but the idea that these were places where luxury items were made continued. Usually the still-room was in the housekeeper's part of the house, rather than the cook's. Here jams, jellies, syrups and sauces, and the newly fashionable chutneys and pickles were made and kept under lock and key. Good examples of nineteenth-century still-rooms can be seen at Uppark and Petworth, both in Sussex, and at Tatton Park in Cheshire.

These arrangements were echoed right down the social scale, so that the humblest cottage might boast a jam cupboard, using the rich harvests of summer to brighten the dull culinary months, and to provide foodstuffs such as pickled damsons, rhubarb jam and quince cheese for the celebration of Christmas and other special occasions.

The recipes included in this book reflect this range. Some come from the archives of country houses, such as the family papers of the Yorkes at Erddig in Wales or the Drydens of Canons Ashby in Northamptonshire. Others have been handed down through generations of housewives. Many come from the cooks and chefs at National Trust restaurants and tearooms, who are reviving old traditions and harvesting the produce grown in the gardens and orchards of their properties. This book is dedicated to them for their generosity in sharing their ideas and recipes. Lastly, several of the recipes come from my own family, for which I thank them.

As I have already pointed out, making jam and preserves is not difficult, and many of the edible gifts can be made by beginners. But it is important to remember some basic rules about hygiene. Before you start making any preserve, it is important that all bottles, jars and closures (lids, etc) are clean, free of cracks, and sterile to prevent the growth of moulds and yeasts. Re-used jars and bottles, without proper seals, are suitable for short-term storage only, and are best kept in the refrigerator. For long-term keeping in the store cupboard, be sure to buy new lids for them, or use proper preserving jars and bottles with airtight lids and seals.

To sterilise jars, bottles and lids, first wash them in hot water with detergent, then rinse thoroughly in hot water. Stand the jars and bottles right-side up, on a wire rack in a large saucepan, making sure that they don't touch either the sides of the pan or each other. Pour in enough water to cover them completely, then bring to the boil. Boil rapidly for 10 minutes, then remove from the water and stand upside down on a clean, thick tea-towel to drain. Using a pair of tongs, dip the lids in the boiling water, then leave to dry thoroughly on the tea-towel. Dry the sterilised jars and bottles in a preheated oven at 110°C/225°F, right side up, on a baking sheet for about 15 minutes. (They can be kept warm in the oven until required or, if the preserve is to be put into a cold container, remove them, leave to cool and fill as soon as possible.)

Always pot preserves straight from the pan or when totally cold: never when just hot or warm because this will lead to condensation and mould on the preserve.

At the beginning of each chapter I have listed the basic equipment needed with the method of preservation, but the most worthwhile investment for the avid preserve-maker is a good quality preserving pan – a wide, fairly shallow pan of good quality stainless steel is best. A sugar thermometer and a jam funnel for pouring jams and chutneys from one container to another are also very useful, but the other items are pieces of everyday equipment.

I have already thanked the cooks and my family for their ideas and recipes, but there are many others who have contributed to this book. The photographs, which I hope will inspire you to heights of culinary achievement, were taken in the fine Victorian kitchens and larders at Lanhydrock in Cornwall by Andreas von Einsiedel and Philip Harris. Such a shoot always involves a lot of backstage work, and I would also like to mention Graham Scotland, the restaurant manager at Lanhydrock, the cooks, Alison Pearn and Barbara Trewin who made the biscuits and sweets, Andrea Marchington and Ken Golding who put up with all the disruption, and Jeremy Pearson who tied the parcels with such panache. Most of the edible delights shown in the photographs were made specially, but the candied fruits were brought in for us from Portugal by Clements & Companhia of Spitalfields in London. Lastly I would like to thank Sophie Blair, Morwenna Wallis and Margaret Willes in the National Trust's publishing office.

CHAPTER 1

Chutneys

Chutneys are Asian in origin, coming from the Hindustani word 'chatni' meaning a strong, sweet relish. They first appeared in Britain, together with ketchups or spicy sauces, at the end of the seventeenth century as a result of increased trade through the East India Company. One of the earliest examples to be introduced was 'Piccalilli', an elaborate Indian pickle, adopted by English cooks as early as 1694. Pieces of cabbage, cauliflower, celery and other vegetables were placed in a brine and vinegar sauce, flavoured with ginger, garlic, pepper, bruised mustard seed and powdered turmeric.

Chutneys existed in their oriental form until the nineteenth century. Then, the fashion-conscious cooks of English families started to make their own 'chatnis' and relishes based on the exotic oriental recipes. They cooked green peaches, mangoes and bananas with onions, garlic and chillies, and mixed these with fresh, salted or smoked fish, salt, olive oil and vinegar. These 'chatnis' were served with 'currie', cutlets, steak, pork, cold meats or fish. Soon, however, the taste for chutneys developed and many different recipes were introduced using home-grown produce, such as plums, apples, damsons, and particularly tomatoes. These proved to be excellent. The olive oil was omitted, sugar added and they became milder in taste, more like our modern chutneys.

Today, chutney is a sweet and sour condiment to accompany cold meats, fish, pies, curries and cheese. It is made from a mixture of fruit and/or vegetables cooked to a pulp with sugar, spices, salt and vinegar. The salt, sugar and vinegar are the preservatives.

Many National Trust restaurants and tea rooms make their own chutneys to serve with local cheeses, cold meats and fish. Wherever possible, vegetables, herbs and fruit from the estate are used.

To make Chutney

Equipment Needed:

1 An aluminium, aluminium-coated, stainless steel or enamelled cast-iron preserving pan, or large saucepan. Vinegar will corrode pans of brass, copper or iron.
2 Clean and dry heat-proof jars with airtight vinegar-proof lids, or jam-pot covers.

Choosing and Preparing the Vegetables and Fruit:

1 Vegetables and fruit for chutney can be soft and slightly over-ripe, but must be sound.
2 Peel and chop finely, mince or process, cutting out and discarding any bad parts. Onions, garlic and other ingredients, which need long cooking to tenderise them, can initially be cooked separately in water, as sugar and vinegar tend to harden rather than soften them.

Choosing the Vinegar and Sugar:

1 Any type of vinegar can be used, depending on the flavour and colour required for the finished chutney, but always use good-quality vinegar.
2 Brown sugars give rich colours and heavier flavours than white. If you want a pale-coloured chutney, add the sugar near the end of the cooking with some of the vinegar. Black treacle and honey make good alternative sweeteners. Dried fruit also adds sweetness as well as texture and colour.

Choosing the Spices:

1 Spices can be whole or ground. Ground spice is easier to handle, but whole spice gives the chutney a better flavour as it retains its volatile oil during storage.
2 When whole spices are used, they should be bruised and tied in a small square of muslin and removed before potting.

Cooking and Potting the Chutney:

1 Cook the vegetables and/or fruit with the sugar, vinegar and spices very slowly, un-covered, until the mixture has thickened and all the excess liquid has evaporated, stirring frequently. This can take from 1-4 hours, but usually $1^1/_2$-2 hours is long enough. Generally the longer a chutney is cooked, the more mellow the flavour and the darker the colour. To tell when a chutney is cooked, make a channel right across the surface with a wooden spoon and if this does not fill with vinegar, then it is ready.
2 While still hot, spoon into prepared jars up to the rim and cover.
3 Label and date the pots, then store in a cool, dry, dark cupboard. It is usually best to allow chutney to mature for at least 3 months.

Cliveden's Apple Chutney

The cook for the restaurant in the Old Conservatory at Cliveden, on the banks of the Thames, makes her own apple chutney using this classic recipe.

Metric	US	Imperial	
225g	8oz	8oz	onions, peeled and finely chopped
675g	1½lb	1½lb	cooking apples, peeled, cored and roughly chopped
600ml	2½ cups	1 pint	malt vinegar
125g	¾ cup	4oz	sultanas
15g	4tsp	½oz	mixed spice
15g	2tbsp	½oz	sea salt
350g	1¾ cups	12oz	soft brown sugar
5ml	1tsp	1tsp	ground ginger

Cook the chopped onions in boiling water for 5 minutes to soften them, then drain. Place all the other ingredients in a large pan, and add the drained onions. Bring to the boil very slowly, stirring frequently to dissolve the sugar. Simmer for 1½–2 hours, until thick, stirring occasionally to prevent sticking. Pour into prepared jars, cover and store for at least 1 month before using.

Apple, Onion and Sage Chutney

This is a light, fruity chutney flavoured with sage, which is particularly good with pork and poultry. It is one of several that the restaurant at Trerice, a small Elizabethan manor house near Newquay in Cornwall, make in their own kitchen and sell to visitors. They also make a version using mint instead of sage.

Metric	US	Imperial	
1·35kg	3lb	3lb	cooking apples, peeled, cored and chopped
1·35kg	3lb	3lb	onions, finely chopped
450g	1lb	1lb	sultanas
			grated rind and juice of 2 lemons
675g	2¾ cups	1½lb	demerara sugar
600ml	2½ cups	1 pint	malt vinegar
60ml	¼ cup	4tbsp	chopped fresh sage

Place all the ingredients, except the sage, in a large saucepan. Cook as for Cliveden's Apple Chutney (see above), then stir in the sage. Pot, seal and leave to mature for 2–3 months.

Banana and Apple Chutney

The passion for growing tender exotic fruit against all the odds of the English climate meant that much money and effort went into growing pineapples, melons and even bananas. At Petworth House in Sussex, Henry Wyndham, 2nd Lord Leconfield, is said to have built a special glasshouse in the mid-nineteenth century and sent his head gardener to Kew Gardens to learn how to grow bananas, in the belief that the fruit tasted much better straight from the tree. Leconfield was disgusted to find that, having spent £3000 on producing it, his first banana tasted exactly like any other. This is a typical nineteenth-century recipe.

Metric	US	Imperial	
1·8kg	4lb	4lb	cooking apples, peeled, cored and finely chopped
12	12	12	bananas, peeled and sliced thinly
450g	1lb	1lb	onions, peeled and finely chopped
225g	1 cup	8oz	seedless raisins
15ml	1 tbsp	1 tbsp	salt
5ml	1 tsp	1 tsp	dry mustard
5ml	1 tsp	1 tsp	ground ginger
5ml	1 tsp	1 tsp	ground cinnamon
15ml	1 tbsp	1 tbsp	curry powder
1·2 litres	5 cups	2 pints	malt vinegar
450g	2 cups	1lb	granulated sugar

Place all the ingredients except the vinegar and sugar in a large pan. Pour on half the vinegar, then bring slowly to the boil and simmer for about 30 minutes. Add the remaining vinegar and the sugar, then cook and pot as for Cliveden's Apple Chutney (see page 11). Leave to mature for at least 1 month.

Spiced Blackberry Chutney

This chutney has a delicious fruity flavour. Try to pick the larger berries if possible as they are juicier. The chutney is sieved after cooking to remove the pips.

Metric	US	Imperial	
1·35kg	3lb	3lb	blackberries
450g	1lb	1lb	cooking apples, peeled cored and chopped
450g	1lb	1lb	onions, finely chopped
15ml	1tbsp	1tbsp	cooking salt
15g	4tsp	1/2oz	dry mustard
25g	2tbsp	1oz	ground ginger
5ml	1tsp	1tsp	ground mace
2·5ml	1/2tsp	1/2tsp	cayenne pepper
600ml	21/2 cups	1 pint	white wine vinegar
450g	21/4 cups	1lb	soft brown sugar

Pick over and wash the blackberries. Put all the ingredients except the sugar in a large pan. Bring to the boil and cook gently for about 1 hour until soft. Push the chutney through a nylon sieve and return to the pan. Stir in the sugar, then heat gently until it has completely dissolved. Bring to the boil, then reduce the heat and simmer gently for about 30 minutes, or until thick. Pour into prepared jars, cover and leave to mature for 2–3 months.

Polesden Lacey's Courgette Chutney

This recipe was provided by the chef at the restaurant at Polesden Lacey near Dorking in Surrey. He recommends enjoying the chutney with home-made bread, fruit and fine conversation.

Metric	US	Imperial	
2·75kg	6lb	6lb	courgettes
40ml	21/2 tbsp	21/2 tbsp	salt
900g	2lb	2lb	tomatoes, skinned and chopped
450g	1lb	1lb	onions, chopped
900g	2lb	2lb	sultanas
			rind of 4 oranges
1·8kg	4lb	4lb	caster sugar
600ml	21/2 cups	1 pint	red wine vinegar
600ml	21/2 cups	1 pint	malt vinegar
15g	4tsp	1/2oz	ground cinnamon

Chop the courgettes into rings and sprinkle with salt. Stand for about two hours to allow them to sweat, then wash and dry.

Put all the ingredients into a pan and simmer on a low heat, stirring from time to time. When the mixture has thickened, pour into prepared jars, cover and store for at least 1 month before using.

Cragside's Curried Fruit Chutney

This is served in the Vickers Restaurant at Cragside, the imposing Victorian country house built by Sir William, later Lord, Armstrong at Rothbury in Northumberland.

Metric	US	Imperial	
450g	1lb	1lb	dried apricots
450g	1lb	1lb	dried peaches
450g	1lb	1lb	dates, stoned
450g	1lb	1lb	raisins
3-4	3-4	3-4	cloves, crushed
450g	2¼ cups	1lb	soft, light brown sugar
600ml	2½ cups	1 pint	white malt vinegar
600ml	2½ cups	1 pint	water
10ml	2tsp	2tsp	salt
10ml	2tsp	2tsp	mild curry powder

Chop or mince the dried fruit coarsely (this can be done in a food processor). Place all the ingredients in a pan and heat gently until the sugar has completely dissolved, then bring to the boil. Cover and simmer for 15-20 minutes, before potting (see page 10). Store for at least 1 month to allow the chutney to mature before eating.

Spiced Damson and Raisin Chutney

A number of interesting damson trees are grown in the orchard at Hardwick Hall in Derbyshire, including a variety called Merryweather, which comes, like the Bramley apple, from the nearby town of Southwell in Nottinghamshire. Although a traditional Northern treat, damsons also grow well in the West Country. Serve this spicy chutney with cold meats, particularly ham and pork, poultry and game, raised pies and cheese.

Metric	US	Imperial	
1·35kg	3lb	3lb	damsons
450g	1lb	1lb	cooking apples, peeled, cored and finely chopped
450g	1lb	1lb	onions, peeled and finely chopped
3	3	3	cloves garlic, crushed
10ml	2tsp	2tsp	ground ginger
450g	3 cups	1lb	seedless raisins
450g	2¼ cups	1lb	dark soft brown sugar
450g	2 cups	1lb	demerara sugar
1·2 litres	5 cups	2pints	malt vinegar
30ml	2tbsp	2tbsp	salt
10ml	2tsp	2tsp	whole cloves
1	1	1	cinnamon stick
25g	2tbsp	1oz	whole allspice berries

Wash the damsons removing any stalks, then place them in a large pan. Cook very gently in their own juice until tender, then remove the stones. Add all the other ingredients except the cloves, cinnamon and allspice and stir thoroughly. Tie the spices in a square of muslin and place in the pan. Cook and pot as for Cliveden's Apple Chutney (see page 11), removing the muslin bag of spices at the end of cooking. Leave to mature for at least 3 months.

Elderberry Chutney

Elderberries are such a versatile fruit and free to everyone if you can beat the birds. In this chutney the elderberries are sieved after the initial cooking to remove their pips. Serve with cheese, cold meats or raised pies.

Metric	US	Imperial	
900g	2lb	2lb	elderberries
450g	1lb	1lb	cooking apples, peeled, cored and finely chopped
450g	1lb	1lb	onions, chopped
450g	3 cups	1lb	seedless raisins
5ml	1tsp	1tsp	ground cinnamon
5ml	1tsp	1tsp	paprika
5ml	1tsp	1tsp	ground ginger
1·25ml	¼tsp	¼tsp	cayenne pepper
225g	1 cup	8oz	granulated sugar
300ml	1¼ cups	½ pint	distilled malt vinegar

Carefully strip the elderberries from their stalks then wash well. Cook gently for 10-15 minutes until soft, then pass the berries and their juice through a nylon sieve into a bowl to remove the pips. Pour the elderberry pulp into a pan with all the other ingredients, then cook and pot as for Cliveden's Apple Chutney (see page 11). Store for at least 1 month before using.

Killerton Gooseberry Chutney

The restaurant and tea room at Killerton, in Devon, the home of the Aclands, are famous for their home-made gooseberry chutney which accompanies delicious West Country cheeses, locally smoked fish and bread, freshly baked in their kitchen. Make this recipe when gooseberries are cheap – unripe green fruit is best.

Metric	US	Imperial	
1·1 kg	2¹/₂lb	2¹/₂lb	gooseberries, topped and tailed
300ml	1¹/₄ cups	¹/₂ pint	malt or white wine vinegar
125g	³/₄ cup	4oz	raisins
125g	³/₄ cup	4oz	sultanas
1	1	1	large onion, finely chopped
450g	2¹/₄ cups	1lb	soft brown sugar
			pinch of turmeric
15g	4tsp	¹/₂oz	ground black pepper
			mixed spice and cinnamon combined

Wash and top and tail the gooseberries, place in a large pan. Cook in the vinegar until soft and pulpy, then add all other ingredients. Cook and pot as for Cliveden's Apple Chutney (see page 11). Leave to mature for 2-3 months.

Chutneys and pickles: Hidcote's Red Tomato and Ginger Chutney, Runner Bean Pickle, Oxburgh's Sweet Cucumber Pickle, and Cliveden's Apple Chutney. (*NTPL/Andreas von Einsiedel*)

Marrow, Red Tomato and Date Chutney

This is an inexpensive recipe for using up a harvest festival marrow or a glut of tomatoes. The chutney is especially good with hamburgers and hot dogs.

Metric	US	Imperial	
1·35kg	3lb	3lb	marrow
75g	5tbsp	3oz	salt
900g	2lb	2lb	red tomatoes
225g	8oz	8oz	onions
350g	12oz	12oz	cooking apples
600ml	2½ cups	1 pint	distilled malt vinegar
225g	8oz	8oz	cooking dates, stoned and chopped
450g	2¼ cups	1lb	soft light brown sugar
15ml	1tbsp	1tbsp	mustard seeds
30ml	2tbsp	2tbsp	ground ginger
10ml	2tsp	2tsp	ground allspice
			large pinch of freshly grated nutmeg

Peel the marrow and cut it in half. Scoop out the seeds and discard them, then cut the flesh into 1·25cm/½in cubes. Put these into a bowl, sprinkling each layer with salt. Cover the bowl and leave for 24 hours.

The next day, rinse the salted marrow under cold running water, drain well and set aside. Skin and chop the tomatoes, peel and chop the onions and peel, core and slice the apples. Put the tomatoes, onions and apples in a large preserving pan. Add the vinegar, stir well, then bring to the boil over a moderate heat. Reduce the heat and cook gently for 30 minutes. Add the dates, sugar and spices, followed by the reserved marrow. Stir well and bring to the boil over a moderate heat.

Reduce the heat. Cook and pot as for Cliveden's Apple Chutney (see page 11). Store for 2–3 months to allow the chutney to mature before eating.

VARIATION

Courgette, Pumpkin or Squash Chutney Substitute pumpkin or squash for the marrow and prepare in the same way. Courgettes will need only to be trimmed before being cut into pieces.

One of the dressers in the late Victorian Dry Larder at Lanhydrock.
(*NTPL/Andreas von Einsiedel*)

Pear, Orange and Ginger Chutney

Quinces or apples could be used in this chutney, but it is very good with pears. This is another recipe from Trerice Restaurant, where the cooks make it with local Cornish varieties of pear from the estate orchard.

Metric	US	Imperial	
1·35kg	3lb	3lb	cooking pears, peeled, cored and roughly chopped
225g	8oz	8oz	onions, finely chopped
225g	1½ cups	8oz	stoned raisins, chopped
50g	2oz	2oz	stem ginger, finely chopped
350g	1¾ cups	12oz	demerara sugar
400ml	1½ cups	¾ pint	white wine vinegar
			grated rind and juice of 2 oranges
15g	½oz	½oz	dried root ginger
15g	½oz	½oz	whole cloves

Put the pears, onions and raisins in a large pan with the other ingredients except the root ginger and cloves. Tie these in a small square of muslin, then add to the pan. Cook and pot as for Cliveden's Apple Chutney (see page 11). Store for 6 months, if possible, before using.

Spiced Plum and Lime Chutney

Metric	US	Imperial	
2kg	4½lb	4½lb	cooking plums, stoned and roughly chopped
2	2	2	large onions, finely chopped
5	5	5	garlic cloves, chopped
2	2	2	fresh chillies, seeded and chopped
			grated rind and juice of 2 limes
			grated rind and juice of 1 lemon
5cm	2in	2in	piece of fresh root ginger, peeled and grated
600ml	2½ cups	1 pint	wine vinegar
500g	2½ cups	1lb 2oz	demerara sugar
2	2	2	sticks of cinnamon
25g	1oz	1oz	allspice berries
5ml	1tsp	1tsp	black peppercorns

Place the plums in a large pan with all the other ingredients except the cinnamon, allspice berries and peppercorns. Grind these spices in a spice mill or pestle and mortar until you have a fine powder. Add to the pan, then cook and pot as for Cliveden's Apple Chutney (see page 11). Store for at least 2 months before using.

VARIATIONS

Spiced Damson and Lime Chutney Substitute damsons for plums.

Plum, Lime and Coriander Chutney Replace berries with 30ml/2tbsp coriander seeds.

Spiced Pumpkin and Raisin Chutney

An excellent way of using up the flesh after making a pumpkin lantern for Halloween. Any variety of squash can be used in the same way.

Metric	US	Imperial	
1·35kg	2½lb	2½lb	pumpkin flesh, chopped
900g	4¼ cups	2lb	brown or white sugar
225g	1 cup	8oz	seedless raisins
600ml	2½ cups	1 pint	distilled malt vinegar
125g	4oz	4oz	onion, peeled and chopped
1·25ml	¼tsp	¼tsp	freshly grated nutmeg
25g	2tbsp	1oz	salt
5ml	1tsp	1tsp	ground ginger
5ml	1tsp	1tsp	freshly ground black pepper
			juice of 1 lemon
30ml	2tbsp	2tbsp	grape juice
4	4	4	bay leaves

Place the pumpkin flesh in a large bowl with all the other ingredients. Stir well, then cover and leave to one side for 3 hours. Transfer to a preserving pan, then cook and pot as for Cliveden Apple Chutney (see page 11). Store for about 1 month to improve the flavour before eating.

Rhubarb and Coriander Chutney

George Wyndham, 3rd Earl of Egremont, was amongst the earliest cultivators of rhubarb as a garden plant at Petworth in the eighteenth century. It took another hundred years to become established as the carefully nurtured plant of Victorian kitchen gardens, where it was forced under tall terracotta pots. This chutney recipe belongs to Victorian times, but is invaluable for making inroads into a late-season glut of rhubarb which is no longer delicate enough for enticing desserts.

Metric	US	Imperial	
450g	1 lb	1 lb	onions, finely chopped
900g	2 lb	2 lb	trimmed rhubarb, cut into short lengths
400ml	1½ cups	¾ pint	red wine vinegar or raspberry vinegar (see page 45)
7.5ml	1½ tsp	1½ tsp	salt
225g	1½ cups	8oz	seedless raisins
225g	1½ cups	8oz	sultanas
10ml	2 tsp	2 tsp	curry powder
175g	1¾ cups	6oz	granulated sugar
15g	4 tsp	½ oz	whole coriander seeds

Cook the chopped onions in a little boiling water until tender, then drain. Place the rhubarb in a pan with all the other ingredients except the coriander seeds. Lightly bruise these, then tie in a square of muslin, and add to the pan. Cook and pot as for Cliveden's Apple Chutney (see page 11). Allow to mature for at least 1 month before eating. Serve with curries and spicy dishes, or with cold meats and cheese.

Wimpole's Spring Rhubarb, Melon and Ginger Chutney

The kitchen garden at Wimpole Hall near Cambridge grows the rhubarb for this unusual chutney, which was invented by the restaurant chef to serve with locally smoked fish and poultry.

Metric	US	Imperial	
4	4	4	garlic cloves, crushed with a little salt
125g	4oz	4oz	red onion, finely chopped
600ml	2½ cups	1 pint	distilled malt vinegar
900g	2 lb	2 lb	forced rhubarb, washed and cut into 2·5cm/1in lengths
1	1	1	medium Honeydew melon, peeled and seeded and cut into 1cm/½in cubes
175g	6oz	6oz	preserved stem ginger, sliced
125g	½ cup	4oz	soft brown sugar
150ml	⅔ cup	¼ pint	stem ginger juice

Boil the garlic and onion with the vinegar until it has reduced by half. Simmer the rhubarb, melon and ginger with the sugar and ginger juice until the rhubarb is tender, but not broken up.

Strain the fruit through a sieve, reserving the juices. Add the juice to the vinegar and boil together until reduced to a syrup (taking care not to burn). Add the fruits to this syrup and bring back to the boil. Spoon into prepared jars, then seal and store for at least 1 month before using.

Hidcote's Red Tomato and Ginger Chutney

A speciality of Hidcote Garden Restaurant in Gloucestershire, where it is served with a platter of local cheeses and bread freshly baked in their kitchen.

Metric	US	Imperial	
4	4	4	large onions, finely chopped
1·35kg	3lb	3lb	tomatoes, skinned and chopped
450g	1lb	1lb	cooking apples, peeled, cored and finely chopped
450g	1lb	1lb	carrots, peeled and finely chopped
20ml	4tsp	4tsp	fresh root ginger, peeled and grated
4	4	4	cloves garlic, crushed
225g	1¼ cups	8oz	sultanas
10ml	2tsp	2tsp	salt
10ml	2tsp	2tsp	mixed spice
900ml	4 cups	1½ pints	malt vinegar
800g	3 cups	1lb 12oz	demerara sugar

Cook the chopped onions in a little water until tender, then drain well. Place in a large pan with all the other ingredients except the sugar, then bring to the boil and simmer for about 30 minutes, or until the carrots are tender. Add the sugar and continue to cook until it has dissolved completely. Pot as for Cliveden's Apple Chutney (see page 11). Leave to mature for 2–3 months.

Red Tomato Chow-Chow

This chutney is based on a recipe from Mrs Beeton's *Book of Household Management*, published in 1861, when tomato recipes were finding their way into most cookery books, having been regarded with great suspicion since their introduction in Tudor times. They had been christened 'love-apples' as they were regarded as an aphrodisiac, which of course prevented their consumption by 'polite society'.

Metric	US	Imperial	
2·75kg	6lb	6lb	large, ripe tomatoes
450g	1lb	1lb	onions, finely chopped
3	3	3	garlic cloves, finely chopped
3	3	3	green peppers, seeded and finely sliced
3	3	3	red peppers, seeded and finely sliced
400ml	1½ cups	¾ pint	white wine vinegar
225g	1¼ cups	8oz	soft brown sugar
50g	½ cup	2oz	cooking salt
5ml	1 tsp	1 tsp	paprika
			grated rind and juice of 2 lemons
			grated rind and juice of 1 orange
5ml	1 tsp	1 tsp	ground mace
5ml	1 tsp	1 tsp	ground black pepper
5ml	1 tsp	1 tsp	ground ginger
			pinch of cayenne pepper

Scald and peel the tomatoes, then cut them in half and squeeze into a bowl to remove most of the seeds. Put the tomato flesh into a large pan and add the strained juice of the tomatoes. (This is only to remove excess seeds from the chutney as they do not look very appetising. If they don't worry you, don't bother.) Add all the other ingredients. Cook and pot as for Cliveden's Apple Chutney (see page 11). Store for several months if possible before using.

Green Tomato and Mint Chutney

The Victorians regarded this as an ideal relish for cold meats and cheese, whether made with or without mint.

Metric	US	Imperial	
350g	12oz	12oz	onions, finely chopped
1·35kg	3lb	3lb	green tomatoes, chopped
350g	12oz	12oz	cooking apples, peeled, cored and finely chopped
900ml	4 cups	1½ pints	Pickling Vinegar (see page 48)
350g	1¾ cups	12oz	white or brown sugar
2	2	2	garlic cloves, crushed
175g	1 cup	6oz	seedless raisins
30ml	2 tbsp	2 tbsp	cooking salt
7·5ml	1½ tsp	1½ tsp	chopped fresh mint

Cook the chopped onions in a little water until tender, then drain well. Place in a large pan with all the other ingredients except the mint. Cook as for Cliveden's Apple Chutney (see page 11). Stir in the chopped mint, then pot and cover. Leave to mature for 2-3 months.

Uncooked Chutney

Felicity Richards, mother of the manager of the tea-room at Mottisfont Abbey Garden near Romsey in Hampshire, invented this recipe. It has now become popular in other National Trust restaurants in the area. The chutney can be used immediately, but does improve in flavour if kept for a few months.

Metric	US	Imperial	
450g	1lb	1lb	cooking apples, peeled and cored
450g	3 cups	1lb	sultanas
450g	1lb	1lb	onions, peeled
450g	1lb	1lb	cooking dates, stoned
450g	2½ cups	1lb	soft brown sugar
600ml	2½ cups	1 pint	malt or white wine vinegar
15ml	1tbsp	1tbsp	sea salt
5ml	1tsp	1tsp	ground cloves
5ml	1tsp	1tsp	ground allspice
1·25ml	¼tsp	¼tsp	cayenne pepper
5ml	1tsp	1tsp	ground coriander
50g	2oz	2oz	fresh root ginger, peeled and finely chopped

Process or mince the apples, sultanas, onions and dates together and place in a large china or glass bowl. Stir in the remaining ingredients, then cover with a clean cloth and leave for 24 hours.

Taste and adjust the seasonings as necessary, then spoon into sterilised jars or into plastic tubs. Store in the refrigerator.

CHAPTER 2

Pickles

Pickling is one of the most ancient methods of preserving fruit and vegetables. The Romans were very keen on pickling to preserve a part of their fruit and vegetable harvest using vinegar from wine that had gone flat. Wine vinegar remained popular right up to the nineteenth century for pickles and chutneys, which is why pickles used to have a milder flavour than our modern ones made with malt vinegar. We are now beginning to rediscover the taste for pickling with wine vinegar.

Vines were re-introduced to England in medieval times by monks, and the grapes which remained unripe at the end of the season were fermented to form 'verjuice', a kind of sharp vinegar used in pickling. Where grapes were not available, crab apples were also made into verjuice for preservatives, but the variety of pickles was limited by the produce available. As the variety increased in the sixteenth and seventeenth centuries, so pickling grew in popularity. Pickled vegetables, herbs, walnuts, flowers and fruit added colour and flavour to fresh salads, meat and fish dishes, and also supplied winter salads.

In the latter part of the seventeenth century, the East India Company imported new fruits and the variety of pickles grew ever larger. Jars of pickled mangoes were copied using home-grown melons, cucumbers, peaches, onions or plums. By the end of the nineteenth century most of today's pickle manufacturers were established. A number of the old recipes have disappeared, but many of the National Trust restaurants are now making their own pickles and hope to re-introduce some that have been long-forgotten. I have included some of these recipes in this chapter.

To Make Pickles

There are basically three types of pickles: clear, sweet and mustard.

Equipment Needed

1 An aluminium, aluminium-coated or stainless steel preserving pan or large saucepan.
2 Heat proof, wide-mouthed jars with vinegar-proof, airtight covers. Vinegar corrodes bare metal lids and this will taint and discolour your pickle, so make sure any metal lids have plastic-coated linings, or use plastic covers. If your lids are not airtight, the vinegar will evaporate quickly.
3 A large china or glass bowl to hold the vegetables in brine.

Choosing and Preparing the Vegetables and Fruit

1 Use only young fresh vegetables or perfect, just-ripe fruit.
2 Cut into suitably sized pieces if necessary, cutting out and discarding any bad parts.
3 Vegetables are usually soaked in brine or layered with dry cooking salt before bottling. This draws out the moisture from the tissues which would dilute the vinegar and reduce its preservative quality. If you want a very crisp pickle, dry salting is best. Rinse off excess salt from the vegetables and drain thoroughly.
4 Fruit is usually cooked in sweetened, spiced vinegar before bottling. Prick the skins of whole fruit before cooking or they may shrivel.
5 Pack the prepared vegetables or fruit into clean, dry jars without squashing or bruising them. Any excess water in the jar can be drained out.

Completing the Pickle

1 Choose a good-quality vinegar and one which suits the particular pickle you are making. For example, if you want to preserve the colour of a certain vegetable, like red cabbage, it is a good idea to use a white vinegar, whereas eggs are better pickled with the stronger-flavoured malt vinegar.
2 Flavour your vinegar with herbs and spices. It is a good idea to have a ready supply of Pickling Vinegar (see page 48) rather than having to make it up at the last minute.
3 Pour the spiced vinegar or syrup over the pickles in the jars to cover them by at least 1cm/½in. The vegetables or fruit tend to absorb the liquid and those at the top may become exposed, so you may have to top up the vinegar after a few days. Use cold vinegar unless a soft pickle is preferred, for example for walnuts or damsons, when boiling vinegar should be added, making sure the jars are warm.

Covering and Storing the Jars

1 Cover your pickles carefully and label and date the jars.
2 Store in a cool, dark place to preserve their colour and flavour. Pickles should be kept for a short while for the flavours to mellow before being used. The exception to this is red cabbage which need only be kept for 1 week, and will go soft if kept for longer than 3 months.

Pickled Crab Apples

This was probably the first fruit pickle ever made in Britain. It certainly dates back to Roman times and may go back even further as crab apples were one of the first fruits eaten by prehistoric man. We tend to ignore them nowadays, but they are still a very useful fruit for pickling and jellying with their rather sharp taste.

Metric	US	Imperial	
1·35kg	3lb	3lb	crab apples
			pared rind of ½ lemon
600ml	2½ cups	1 pint	Sweet Pickling Vinegar made with white wine vinegar (see page 49)

Choose crab apples of even size, if possible, and wash them. Remove any stalks and dry the apples thoroughly. Prick all over with a darning needle or skewer. Put the pared lemon rind and vinegar into a saucepan and bring to the boil. Add the apples and cook gently until almost tender.

Use a draining spoon to remove the fruit and pack carefully into hot jars. Discard the lemon peel from the vinegar and boil rapidly for 5 minutes. Pour over the apples and seal at once. Store for 4-6 weeks before using. Serve with cold ham, pork, venison, duck or goose.

Pickled Baby Beets with Horseradish

The very small beetroot (the thinning from the crop) are sweet and delicious. Pickle them whole or slice them thinly. They are very good flavoured with horseradish , but any spiced vinegar will do.

baby beets
a few juniper berries, crushed
Horseradish Vinegar (see page 42)
cooking salt

Heat the oven to 180°C, 350°F, gas mark 4. Wash the beets carefully, taking care not to damage skins or they will lose their lovely colour. Wrap in foil and bake for 1½-2 hours, until tender. Cool, then peel them. Pack them in a wide-mouthed jar with a few crushed juniper berries.

Cover with the vinegar to which you add 15g/½oz/½oz cooking salt for every 600ml/2½cups/1pint vinegar, stirring until it dissolves. Seal and allow to mature for about 1 week, although the pickles will keep for a year without deteriorating. Serve with cold roast beef.

Pickled Beetroot with Lemon or Orange Boil the vinegar with a thinly sliced lemon or orange for 2 minutes. Leave until cold, then strain the vinegar reserving the fruit. Slice the cooked beetroot and pack in jars with the lemon or orange slices. Cover with the cold vinegar.

Spiced Blackberries

Scented with geranium, these spiced fruits are extremely good with cold meats, poultry or soft cream cheeses.

Metric	US	Imperial	
300ml	1¼ cups	½ pint	Pickling Vinegar made with white wine vinegar (see page 48)
450g	2 cups	1lb	sugar
1·35kg	3lb	3lb	large clean blackberries
3	3	3	rose geranium leaves, washed and dried

Gently heat the vinegar with the sugar until the sugar has completely dissolved. Simmer for 5 minutes and then add the blackberries. Simmer for a further 5–6 minutes or until the blackberries are soft, but not disintegrating. Remove the fruit with a draining spoon and pack into warm jars. Boil the vinegar and sugar rapidly for about 5 minutes or until reduced to a thick syrup. Add the geranium leaves to the fruit in the jars and pour over the hot syrup. Seal tightly and store for 2–3 weeks before using.

Pickled Red Cabbage

This was a popular pickle in Tudor and Stuart times because of its glorious colour which looked so attractive in salads. Turnips and beetroot were often added to make 'a pretty pickle'. The restaurant at Baddesley Clinton in Warwickshire makes its own pickled red cabbage to accompany an Elizabethan Salad. The cook recommends using young firm cabbage and preparing it in small batches because it does not keep well.

Metric	US	Imperial	
about 900g	about 2lb	about 2lb	red cabbage
30ml	2 tbsp	2 tbsp	salt
about 600ml	about 2½ cups	about 1 pint	Pickling Vinegar made with white wine or cider vinegar (see page 48)
15ml	1 tbsp	1 tbsp	sugar (optional)
			several slices of raw beetroot
			several slices of onion

Quarter the cabbage, removing outer leaves and centre stalks, as only the heart will make a good pickle. Shred finely and layer it with the salt in a large flat dish or bowl. Cover with a clean cloth and leave to stand overnight.

Dissolve the sugar (if using) in the vinegar and leave until cold. Rinse the salt off the cabbage and drain thoroughly in a sieve. Pack into clean, dry jars and top with a slice of beetroot, for colour, and a slice of onion, for flavour. Pour over the cold vinegar, then cover and seal. Leave for 1 week before eating, but use within 2 months or it will lose its colour and crispness.

VARIATIONS

Pickled White Cabbage Use white cabbage instead of red.

Pickled Red Cabbage and Carrots Wash 225g/8oz/8oz carrots, peel and cut them into matchstick pieces. Layer the carrot and cabbage in the jars and continue as before.

Pickled Red Cabbage with Oranges and Raisins Add the grated rind of 2 oranges, the flesh of the oranges cut into segments and 50g/⅓cup/2oz raisins to the vinegar and sugar. Bring to the boil, then leave until cold. Continue as before.

Oxburgh's Sweet Cucumber Pickle

The restaurant at Oxburgh Hall in Norfolk serves this tasty pickle with a colourful medieval Herb and Flower Salad, the ingredients for which are mostly grown in their kitchen garden. It is also good with home-made crusty bread and farmhouse cheese.

Metric	US	Imperial	
900g	2lb	2lb	cucumbers, diced (unpeeled)
2	2	2	large onions, finely sliced
2	2	2	sticks of celery, finely chopped
25g	¼ cup	1oz	cooking salt
600ml	2½ cups	1 pint	cider vinegar
5ml	1tsp	1tsp	mustard seeds
450g	2¼ cups	1lb	soft brown sugar
2·5ml	½tsp	½tsp	ground turmeric
1·25ml	¼tsp	¼tsp	ground cloves

Put the cucumber, onions and celery in a large china bowl with the salt. Mix well, then cover and leave for 2 hours. Rinse the vegetables under cold running water, then drain well and place in a large pan. Add the vinegar and bring to the boil. Simmer for about 15 minutes, until the vegetables are soft, then add the sugar and spices. Stir until the sugar has completely dissolved, then bring to the boil. Remove from the heat and leave until quite cold. Pot and seal in the usual way. The pickle can be used straight away but improves if kept.

Sweet Damson Pickle

Instead of adding the sugar, you can save time by using Sweet Pickling Vinegar (see page 49), made with white wine or cider vinegar. Plums or greengages can be pickled in the same way, but store for three months before using.

Metric	US	Imperial	
450g	1lb	1lb	large damsons
about 300ml	about 1¼ cups	about ½ pint	white wine or cider vinegar
225g	1 cup	8oz	sugar
			pared rind of ½ lemon
2	2	2	pieces dried root ginger, bruised
1	1	1	blade mace
4	4	4	whole cloves
			cinnamon stick
			blackcurrant leaves

Prick the damsons all over with a darning needle and place in a saucepan. Cover with vinegar and add the sugar. Tie the lemon rind, bruised ginger and other spices in a muslin bag and add to the pan. Cook very gently until the sugar has dissolved, then bring to the boil. Continue to cook very gently until the damsons are just tender, but do not let the skins break.

Place a blackcurrant leaf in the bottom of each warmed jar, then using a draining spoon, transfer the fruit carefully to the jars. Discard the muslin bag and boil the vinegar rapidly for about 5 minutes until reduced to a syrup. Pour immediately over the damsons and cover the jars. They are ready to eat in 4 weeks, but are much better if kept longer. Serve with poultry, particularly duck and goose, game or cold meat.

Sweet Indian Pickle

Piccalilli, or Indian Pickle, was one of the first chutneys to be brought back from the East by the East India Company at the end of the seventeenth century. English cooks adopted the recipe with enthusiasm. A 1765 example at Erddig runs 'Take vinegar one gallon, garlic one pound, ginger one pound, turmeric, mustard seed, long pepper and salt of each 4 ounces'. The garlic had to be peeled and salted for 3 days, then washed and salted again and left for another 3 days, then washed and dried in the sun! All the vegetables to be put into this sauce had to be cut into walnut-sized pieces. The restaurant at Erddig is serving an adaptation of the pickle with local Welsh cheeses.

This sweet version of piccalilli, first introduced in the nineteenth century, is made by the cook for Oxburgh Restaurant using a variety of seasonal vegetables from the kitchen garden. She uses the sharp, hot recipe.

Metric	US	Imperial	
2·75kg	6lb	6lb	prepared vegetables (a mixture of diced cucumber, marrow, courgette, beans, cauliflower florets and small onions)
450g	1lb	1lb	cooking salt
			For Sharp Hot Piccalilli
25-40g	1-1½oz	1-1½oz	dry mustard
25-40g	1-1½oz	1-1½oz	ground ginger
175g	6oz	6oz	white sugar
1 litre	5 cups	2 pints	distilled malt vinegar
20g	¾oz	20g	cornflour
15g	½oz	½oz	ground turmeric
			For Sweet Mild Piccalilli
20g	¾oz	2oz	dry mustard
7·5ml	1½ tsp	1½ tsp	ground ginger
250g	1 cup	9oz	white sugar
1·7 litres	7½ cups	3 pints	distilled malt vinegar
40g	1½oz	1½oz	cornflour
15g	½oz	½oz	ground turmeric

Layer the prepared vegetables on a large plate with the salt and leave overnight covered with a cloth. Next day, drain and rinse the vegetables under cold running water, then dry well. Decide which finish you want, then stir the mustard, ginger and sugar into most of the vinegar. Add the prepared vegetables and simmer until texture is as liked, either crisp or tender. Blend the cornflour and turmeric with the rest of the vinegar and then add to the other ingredients in the pan. Bring to the boil, stirring carefully and boil for 2-3 minutes. Pour into warm jars, cover with a cloth and leave until quite cold, then seal. Store for 2-3 months before eating.

VARIATION

Indian Pickle Omit the sugar from the sauce.

Cotehele's Piccalilli

The restaurant at Cotehele, the romantic medieval manor house on the banks of the River Tamar in Cornwall, serves this piccalilli with a platter of West Country cheeses and home-baked bread. The delicious sauce in the pickle includes curry powder.

Metric	US	Imperial	
450g	1lb	1lb	pickling onions, peeled
675g	1½lb	1½lb	small cauliflower florets
575g	1¼lb	1¼lb	cucumber, cut into 1·25cm/½in dice
450g	1lb	1lb	fine green beans, trimmed and halved
3	3	3	small fresh red chillies, seeded and cut into thin strips
75g	5tbsp	3oz	salt
1·2 litres	5 cups	2 pints	water
			For the Sauce
225g	1 cup	8oz	sugar
75g	½ cup	3oz	plain flour
10ml	2tsp	2tsp	ground allspice
30ml	2tbsp	2tbsp	ground ginger
30ml	2tbsp	2tbsp	mild curry powder
10ml	2tsp	2tsp	ground turmeric
30ml	2tbsp	2tbsp	mustard powder
7·5ml	½tsp	½tsp	cayenne paper
1·2 litres	5 cups	2 pints	distilled malt vinegar
25g	2tbsp	1oz	black peppercorns

Bring the water and salt to the boil in a large pan. Add all the prepared vegetables and cook gently for 5 minutes. Pour into a colander, rinse well under cold water, then drain very well on a clean tea towel.

To make the sauce, put the sugar, flour, allspice, ginger, curry powder, turmeric, mustard and cayenne into a small basin. Add 45-60ml/3-4tbsp of the vinegar and mix to a thick paste. Put this paste with the remaining vinegar and the peppercorns into a pan and bring to the boil, stirring continuously. Reduce the heat and continue to cook, stirring continuously for 3-5 minutes until the sauce thickens. Remove the pan from the heat and leave to cool, stirring occasionally to prevent a skin from forming. Put the drained vegetables into a bowl, add the sauce and mix together. Cover the bowl and leave to stand for 24 hours. The following day, stir the piccalilli again to coat the vegetables evenly, then spoon into clean, dry jars and cover. Store for 2-3 months before eating.

Pickled Mushrooms

Use only the smallest button mushrooms, preferably wild, or at least organically grown so that their flavour is good. They should be white with pale pink gills. Pickle mushrooms in small batches and use up quickly, as they soon deteriorate. An eighteenth-century recipe from Erddig recommends pickling the mushrooms in 'as small Glasses as you can because they soon Decay, when they have taken Air'.

Metric	US	Imperial	
450g	1lb	1lb	small button mushrooms
300ml	1¼ cup	½ pint	white wine vinegar
1	1	1	shallot, peeled and sliced
15ml	1tbsp	1tbsp	root ginger, finely chopped
2	2	2	blades of mace
5ml	1tsp	1tsp	salt
2·5ml	½ tsp	½ tsp	ground black pepper
2·5ml	½ tsp	½ tsp	grated nutmeg
4	4	4	sprigs of fresh thyme
60ml	4tbsp	4tbsp	sherry

Wipe the mushrooms and trim the stalks (use for flavouring soups or stews). Pour the vinegar into a pan and add the remaining ingredients, except for the sherry. Bring to the boil, then simmer for 5 minutes. Add the mushrooms to the boiling vinegar, and bring back to the boil. Cover the pan and simmer for 1 minute until the mushrooms have shrunk slightly. Stir in the sherry, then use a draining spoon to pack the mushrooms into warmed jars and pour in the hot vinegar. Cover at once while still hot, then leave for 1–2 weeks before eating. Use up quickly.

Apple and Thyme Jelly, Strawberry Jam, Blueberry Vinegar, Hazelnut Oil with Peppercorns and Dill, Raspberry Vinegar, Apple and Rosemary Jelly, White Vinegar with Tarragon and Marjoram, Peanut Oil with Garlic, Olive Oil with Garlic, Spices and Chillies, and Sloe Gin. (*NTPL/Andreas von Einsiedel*)

Sweet Pickled Onions

This is the best recipe I have ever used for pickling onions. The resulting onions are sweet and crisp. Do be careful not to cut away too much when you trim the tops and roots of the onions or they will disintegrate and become soggy. Do not worry if any small yellow spots appear on your pickled onions, they are perfectly harmless.

Metric	US	Imperial	
1·35kg	3lb	3lb	small pickling onions, trimmed
50g	2oz	2oz	cooking salt
2–3	2–3	2–3	sprigs of fresh tarragon
1–2	1–2	1–2	green or red fresh chillies, halved
1–1·5 litres	5–7½ cups	2–3 pints	white wine vinegar
350g–450g	1¾–2¼ cups	12–16oz	sugar

Put the onions into a large bowl and cover with boiling water. Leave for about 20 seconds and then pour off the water. Cover with cold water, then peel the onions, keeping them under the water when peeling. Put them into a bowl, sprinkling each layer with salt. Cover with a clean cloth and leave overnight.

Rinse well and shake off as much water as possible. Pack into clean, dry jars, adding a washed sprig of tarragon and half a chilli to each jar.

Boil the vinegar and sugar together for 1 minute, adding 225g/1 cup/8oz sugar to each 750ml/3½ cups/1½ pint vinegar. Pour the hot vinegar over the onions. Cover tightly and store for 2–3 weeks before eating. Use within 6 months.

Jellies on the range in the Victorian Kitchen at Lanhydrock: Herb Garden, Quince, and Spiced Bramble. (*NTPL/Andreas von Einsiedel*)

Spiced Orange Slices

These are delicious served with ham, pork or game. Oranges were preserved in this way in the days when citrus fruit was scarce and expensive.

Metric	US	Imperial	
10 large	10 large	10 large	thin-skinned oranges, cut into 5mm/¼in slices
600ml	2½ cups	1 pint	white wine vinegar
1·1kg	5 cups	2½lb	granulated sugar
1½	1½	1½	cinnamon sticks
8g	¼oz	¼oz	whole cloves
6	6	6	blades of mace

Place the orange slices in a large pan and cover with cold water. Simmer gently, partially covered with a lid, until the peel is tender – about 40 minutes. (The peel should be very soft when pressed between finger and thumb.)

Meanwhile, put all the other ingredients in a pan and boil for a few minutes to make a syrup. Drain the oranges, reserving the liquor and place in the prepared syrup. Simmer, uncovered, for another 30–40 minutes, or until the oranges are translucent. Turn the fruit into a bowl and leave overnight.

Reboil the oranges in the syrup until they are thoroughly cooked. Pack in warm jars, adding syrup to cover and seal. Use the reserved liquor for topping up during storage as the oranges absorb the syrup. Leave for 6–8 weeks before eating. The flavour is even better if left for several more months.

Sweet Pickled Peaches

This recipe dates back to the days when it was fashionable to grow your own peaches, apricots and nectarines. The fruits were very precious and had to be preserved for the winter.

Metric	US	Imperial	
900g	2lb	2lb	firm peaches
			juice of ½ lemon
15ml	1 tbsp	1 tbsp	whole cloves
250ml	1¼ cups	½ pint	Sweet Pickling Vinegar (see page 49) made with white wine or cider vinegar

Place peaches in a bowl and pour boiling water over them. Leave for about 1 minute, then drain. Peel the fruit – the skins will slip off easily. Brush the peaches with lemon juice to prevent them from going brown. Halve and stone, brushing with lemon juice. Crack a few stones, remove and reserve the kernels. Stud each peach with 2–3 cloves.

Put the vinegar in a large pan with the reserved kernels and bring to the boil. Boil for about 5 minutes, then carefully add half the peaches. Simmer very gently until they are just tender, but do not let them disintegrate. Remove the peaches with a draining spoon and place cut sides down in prepared jars. Poach the remaining peaches in the same way and place in jars.

Boil the syrup for about 5 minutes until it has thickened and reduced, then pour it over the peaches. Cover and keep for 1 month before eating. Serve with cold or hot ham, pork, duck or smoked poultry.

VARIATION

Nectarines or apricots can be pickled in the same way, but there is no need to skin apricots.

Spiced Pickled Pears

These are good served with any cold meat, poultry or cheese.

Metric	US	Imperial	
			thinly pared rind and juice of 1 small lemon
10ml	2 tsp	2 tsp	whole cloves
10ml	2 tsp	2 tsp	allspice berries
2	2	2	cinnamon sticks
1	1	1	small piece dried root ginger, bruised
1 litre	4½ cups	1¾ pints	cider or white wine vinegar
150ml	⅔ cup	¼ pint	water
1kg	4¾ cups	2¼ lb	caster sugar
1·3kg	3 lb	3 lb	firm Williams pears, peeled, halved and cored.

Tie the lemon rind and spices in a small piece of muslin. Pour the vinegar, water and lemon juice into a large pan, then add the sugar and bag of spices. Stir over a gentle heat until the sugar has dissolved. Add the pears and bring to the boil, then simmer gently for 15 minutes or until the pears are just tender. Using a slotted spoon, transfer the pears to a colander set over a large bowl and leave to drain.

Discard the bag of spices and boil the syrup for 15 minutes or until reduced by about a third and slightly thickened. Pack the fruit into warm jars and cover with the hot syrup. Cover tightly. Refrigerate any cooled left-over syrup.

After 3 days, open the jars. Pour the syrup into a saucepan and add any reserved syrup. Boil for 3 minutes, then pour the syrup back over the pears. Cover immediately. Label and store for at least 1 month before using.

Spiced Prunes

This preserve can be made at any time of the year. Try to use large succulent prunes; they are very good with cold pork, ham and hot or cold goose or game.

Metric	US	Imperial	
450g	1lb	1lb	large prunes
1·2 litres	5 cups	2 pint	cold, fresh tea
450ml	scant 2 cups	³/₄ pint	red wine vinegar
225g	1 cup	8oz	sugar
5ml	1 tsp	1 tsp	pickling spice, tied in a piece of muslin
			rind of 1 lemon

Soak the prunes overnight in the cold tea. Transfer them to a saucepan with half the remaining soaking liquor and bring to the boil. Cover and simmer very gently for 10–15 minutes or until the prunes are just tender. Drain the prunes, reserving the liquid, and set aside until cold.

Put the vinegar, sugar, muslin bag of spices and lemon rind in a saucepan and heat gently, stirring frequently, until the sugar has dissolved. Bring to the boil and boil rapidly for 5 minutes. Add 250ml/$1^{1}/_{3}$ cups/$^{1}/_{2}$ pint of the reserved cooking liquid from the prunes and bring back to the boil.

Pack the cold prunes into warmed jars and pour the vinegar over them. Cover immediately and store. These prunes can be eaten 24 hours after pickling.

Lemons Preserved in Salt

You use only the skins of preserved lemons, so buy the best and most fragrant organic fruit you can find. Lemons have been preserved in salt for centuries, but have become very fashionable recently. Add to salads, salsas or vinaigrettes, or use in casseroles and sauces.

Metric	US	Imperial	
3	3	3	lemons, preferably unwaxed/organic, quartered lengthwise
75g	³/₄ cup	3oz	sea salt

Pack the lemons as tightly as you can into a 600ml/$2^{1}/_{2}$ cups/1 pint preserving jar. Place the skin sides uppermost and dredge each layer liberally with salt. (If you cannot fit all the lemon quarters into the jar, leave those already packed to stand for about 1 hour until they begin to soften. This makes it easier to press them down, allowing room for the remaining lemon quarters.) Cover with a final layer of salt, then seal the jar.

Leave the lemons for 3–4 weeks to develop their flavour, shaking the jar occasionally to distribute the salt, which eventually dissolves in the juice to form a brine.

To use, take out the required amount of peel and scrape off the flesh. Rinse thoroughly, then slice or chop the softened peel and use as required.

VARIATION

Limes Preserved in Salt Use limes instead of lemons, following the recipe above.

Spiced Quince

This pickled quince is wonderful with ham, pâtés, cured meats and cheese.

Metric	US	Imperial	
1 kg	2¼ lb	2¼ lb	quinces
750 ml	3⅓ cups	1¼ pints	cider vinegar
			pared rind and juice of 1 lemon
10	10	10	whole cloves
20	20	20	black peppercorns, crushed
5 ml	1 tsp	1 tsp	allspice berries, crushed
5 cm	2 in	2 in	piece of fresh root ginger
400 g	2 cups	14 oz	soft brown sugar
1	1	1	cinnamon stick
			cooking salt

Peel, quarter, core and slice the quinces. Put them in a bowl with a splash of the vinegar and the lemon juice to prevent discoloration. Tie the cloves, peppercorns, allspice berries and the root ginger in a piece of muslin. Place this in a pan with the sugar, remaining vinegar, cinnamon stick and lemon peel. Bring to the boil, then simmer gently for 10 minutes. Add the prepared quinces and their juice and simmer over a very gentle heat for about 20 minutes, or until the quinces soften and the syrup has thickened a little. Discard the muslin bag, then add salt to taste. Spoon into prepared jars, cover and seal. The quinces will be ready to eat in 2–3 weeks.

Runner Bean Pickle

I didn't come across this pickle until I moved to Cornwall, where it is very traditional. It is excellent and a marvellous way of coping with a glut of runner beans, which seems to happen to me every year. Do not be tempted to use stringy beans, they must be young and tender.

Metric	US	Imperial	
22·5ml	1½ tbsp	1½ tbsp	English mustard powder
22·5ml	1½ tbsp	1½ tbsp	ground turmeric
22·5ml	1½ tbsp	1½ tbsp	cornflour
900ml	4 cups	1½ pints	malt vinegar
900g	2lb	2lb	runner beans, trimmed and sliced
4	4	4	medium onions, finely sliced
4	4	4	garlic cloves, sliced
15ml	1 tbsp	1 tbsp	cooking salt
675g	2¾ cups	1½ lb	demerara sugar
6	6	6	dried red chillies

Mix the mustard, turmeric and cornflour with a little of the vinegar to make a smooth paste. Place the beans, onions, garlic and salt in a pan and add the remaining vinegar. Simmer until the beans are tender. Stir in the spicy paste, sugar and chillies and heat gently, stirring frequently until the sugar has dissolved. Bring to the boil, stirring, then simmer for 20–30 minutes, or until thick. Spoon the pickle into warmed jars, then cover. Store for 2–3 months before eating.

Pickled Samphire

Marsh samphire, or glasswort, a plant well known to East Anglians, is common on salt marshes around most of the British coast. It has something of the texture and flavour of salty asparagus and makes an excellent pickle, recipes for which appeared in most eighteenth- and nineteenth-century recipe books. An eighteenth-century recipe from Erddig recommends gathering the samphire 'about Midsummer' and pickling it in wine vinegar spiced with 'a little mace, Cloves and Black pepper'. A similar pickle can be made using rock samphire, which grows on rocky coasts and shingle beaches in the south and west of Britain. Both types derive their name from Saint Pierre, or St Peter, the 'rock' of the Christian Church.

The chef at the restaurant of Sissinghurst Castle in Kent pickles samphire in the tradition of country-house kitchens, and serves it with local fish, cold meats and cheese. Samphire is particularly good with cold lamb, traditionally grazed on the salt marshes.

Metric	US	Imperial	
900g	2lb	2lb	samphire
50g	1/2 cup	2oz	cooking salt
1·2 litres	5 cups	2 pints	distilled or dark malt vinegar

Wash and dry the samphire well, then place half in a bowl. Sprinkle with half the salt, then add the remaining samphire and sprinkle with the remaining salt. Cover and leave in a cool place for 24 hours.

Drain the samphire in a colander and rinse well under cold water. Drain, then dry thoroughly and pack into warmed jars. Bring the vinegar to the boil and pour over the samphire, making sure it is completely covered. Cover and leave for at least 1 week before using.

Pickled Vegetables

This pungent pickle is excellent with cold meats and cheese.

Metric	US	Imperial	
1	1	1	medium cauliflower, cut into small florets
1	1	1	medium cucumber, halved, seeded and sliced
1	1	1	red pepper, halved, seeded and cut into 1cm/1/2in squares
1	1	1	green pepper, halved, seeded and cut into 1cm/1/2in squares
175g	6oz	6oz	fine green beans, topped and tailed
175g	6oz	6oz	baby carrots
175g	6oz	6oz	button onions
150g	5oz	5oz	cooking salt
1·7 litres	7 1/2 cups	3 pints	distilled or dark malt vinegar
450g	2 1/4 cups	1lb	sugar
5ml	1 tsp	1 tsp	black peppercorns
5ml	1 tsp	1 tsp	pickling spice

Place all the vegetables together in a large bowl, leaving the baby carrots and button onions whole. Sprinkle with the salt and mix well. Cover and chill for 48 hours.

Meanwhile, make the sweet spiced vinegar. Pour the vinegar into a pan and add the sugar, peppercorns, pickling spice and 7·5ml/1 1/2 tsps/1 1/2 tsps cooking salt. Heat gently until the sugar has dissolved, stirring frequently. Strain through a muslin-lined sieve into a jug, cover and leave until cold.

Rinse the salted vegetables under cold running water, then drain well and pack into jars. Pour in enough spiced vinegar to cover the vegetables completely. Cover and store for at least 2 weeks before using. Use within 2–3 months.

Pickled Green Walnuts

Walnuts are most often planted as specimen trees, rather than as part of an orchard. It is not an indigenous tree, but was introduced into Britain by the Romans. Use walnuts gathered in late June or early July while they are still green and before the shells have begun to form. Remember to wear rubber or disposable polythene gloves while you are preparing them unless you want a pair of beautiful brown hands! Pickled walnuts used to be 'greened' by stewing them in a brass or copper pan so that the vinegar reacted with the metal. An eighteenth-century recipe in the Dryden Family Papers at Canons Ashby in Northamptonshire includes a warning note that this 'greening of them is Apt to make people sick. So better let Alone for it is poisonous'.

Metric	US	Imperial	
450g	1lb	1lb	green walnuts
1·2 litres	5 cups	2 pints	water
125g	1 cup	4oz	cooking salt
about 600ml	about 2¼ cups	about 1 pint	Pickling Vinegar (see page 48)

Prick the walnuts lightly with a darning needle so that the pickle will permeate them. Discard any nuts with hard patches at the end opposite to the stalk, the point where the shell starts to form.

Make a strong brine by mixing half the water and half the salt together in a bowl. Add the walnuts and leave to stand for 3–4 days. Drain the nuts. Mix up another brine using the remaining water and salt. Put the walnuts into this and leave for a further week.

Drain the nuts well, rinse and dry them, then spread them out on a tray or plate. Leave the walnuts in a sunny place for 2 days or until they are completely black, then pack them into clean jars. Heat the pickling vinegar and pour it over the walnuts to cover them completely. Cover tightly when cold and store in a cool, dry place for 6–8 weeks before using.

VARIATION

Sweet Pickled Walnuts Prepare the nuts as above, but cover with Sweet Pickling Vinegar (see page 49).

CHAPTER 3

Flavoured Vinegars and Oils

The Romans introduced the idea of preserving food, including fruits, vegetables, herbs and flowers with vinegar. For the keen cook these are fun to make and produce colourful gifts. They are also so much cheaper than shop-bought varieties and extremely fashionable. Use to flavour sauces, marinades, casseroles and salad dressings.

Choosing the vinegar

Use a good quality vinegar. Malt vinegar can be used to make pickling vinegar for pickles and chutneys, but choose wine, sherry or cider vinegar to make flavoured vinegars for use in salad dressings and for cooking. Champagne vinegar is excellent for making fruit vinegars.

Selecting the flavourings

1 For herb vinegars, use fresh herbs preferably picked before they flower. Lightly crush them on a wooden board with the blade of a large chef's knife, pressing down well with your hands to bring out their aroma. Spices for flavouring vinegars should also be fresh and lightly crushed in a pestle and mortar to release their flavour.
2 Insert the flavourings into a sterilised bottle and add the vinegar to the top.

Sealing and storage

1 Seal the bottle tightly with a non-corrosive, screw-top lid and leave for 2 weeks before using, to allow the flavours to develop.
2 Straining the vinegar through a double layer of muslin after its initial storage will ensure that it lasts longer and becomes clearer. After re-bottling in a freshly sterilised jar, a few fresh ingredients may be added for decoration and identification. Re-seal and use as required.
3 Flavoured vinegars should keep for about 12 months if the vinegar has been strained; if not, the shelf-life will be shorter.

Herb Vinegars

Herb-infused vinegars add punch to salad dressings, marinades and sauces. Basil, bay, chervil, dill, fennel, lemon balm, thyme, tarragon, rosemary, mint, savory, horseradish and garlic can all be used. Purple basil and bronze fennel give stunning rich shades of ruby and burgundy to vinegar.

Pick the herbs on a dry day, and infuse in the vinegar for 2 weeks. Taste for flavour and if you prefer it stronger, strain, reserving the vinegar and repeat with fresh herb leaves. For a decorative effect, add sprigs of the herb.

Garlic Vinegar

Use in marinades and salad dressings and to flavour sauces or mayonnaise.

Metric	US	Imperial	
8	8	8	garlic cloves, peeled
			a little sea salt
600ml	2½ cups	1 pint	white or red wine vinegar

Lightly crush the garlic with a little salt using the flat side of a chef's knife. Place in a large sterilised jar and pour in the vinegar. Seal and shake well. Leave in a sunny place for 2–3 weeks before using, to allow the flavour to develop. Shake the jar every day. Strain through muslin into a sterilised bottle. Seal and use as required.

Horseradish Vinegar

It is an awful job to prepare fresh horseradish, but it does have a much better flavour than dried. Wear rubber gloves and hold the horseradish under water while scrubbing and peeling it, and preferably work in the open air to minimise the eye-burning effect. Use this vinegar for salad dressings and for pickling.

Metric	US	Imperial	
75g	3oz	3oz	fresh horseradish, grated
1	1	1	shallot, peeled and finely chopped
15ml	1 tbsp	1 tbsp	mixed whole peppercorns
2·5ml	½ tsp	½ tsp	cayenne pepper
1·2 litres	5 cups	2 pints	distilled malt vinegar

Put all the ingredients into a bowl or plastic container, cover and leave to stand for 1 week before straining into clean, dry bottles.

Rosemary and Allspice Vinegar

This is excellent in marinades and sauces, especially with lamb, mutton or salmon.

Metric	US	Imperial	
4	4	4	sprigs of fresh rosemary
10ml	2tsp	2tsp	allspice berries
600ml	2½ cups	1 pint	red or white wine vinegar

Strip the rosemary leaves from their stalks. Lightly bruise the leaves by placing the blade of a chef's knife on top of them and pressing down gently with the palm of your hand.

Lightly crush the allspice in a pestle and mortar, or with the end of a rolling pin. Put the rosemary and allspice in a sterilised jar and pour in the vinegar. Cover and shake well. Place on a sunny window ledge, or in a warm place and shake daily for 2-3 weeks. Strain through a double layer of muslin into a sterilised bottle. Cover and use as required.

Sissinghurst's Herb Vinegars

The chef at the restaurant at Sissinghurst makes a great variety of fresh herb vinegars. His method is always the same – he bruises the herbs and spices, then infuses them in the vinegar in a warm place (on the shelves of his kitchen) for 2-3 weeks before straining. Here are just a few of his combinations to inspire you, but do experiment with your own.

Mixed Herb Vinegar
Infuse about 25g/1oz/1oz mixed fresh herbs (for example thyme, tarragon and rosemary), 3 fresh bay leaves, a pinch of fennel seeds and 3 peeled garlic cloves in 600ml/2½ cups/1 pint red or white wine vinegar.

Tarragon and Marjoram
Infuse about 15g/½oz/½oz fresh tarragon and 15g/½oz/½oz fresh marjoram in 600ml/2½ cups/1 pint white wine vinegar.

Tomato and Basil
Infuse about 25g/1oz/1oz fresh basil with 1 beef tomato cut up roughly in 600ml/ 2½ cups/1 pint red or white wine vinegar.

Herb and Shallot
Infuse 2 large sprigs each of rosemary, tarragon, thyme and parsley, 6 black peppercorns, 2 thinly sliced sticks of celery, and 2 thinly sliced shallots in 600ml/2½ cups/ 1 pint white wine vinegar.

Tarragon Vinegar

Perhaps this is the most versatile of all the herb vinegars. Use it to flavour the classic tartar, bearnaise and hollandaise sauces as well as in salad dressings, particularly for pears, tomatoes, chicken and fish.

Metric	US	Imperial	
about 25g	about 1oz	about 1oz	fresh tarragon
600ml	2½ cups	1 pint	white wine vinegar

Lightly bruise the tarragon to release its flavour, then pack it into a sterilised jar. Pour in the vinegar. Seal the jar and shake well. Keep on a sunny window sill or in a warm place for 2–3 weeks before using, to allow the flavours to develop, shaking the jar every day. Strain the vinegar through muslin into a sterilised bottle. Cover and use as required.

Flower Vinegars

These subtle-flavoured vinegars are ideal for using in salad dressings, mayonnaise and marinades. Roses, violets, primroses, cowslips, rosemary or thyme flowers, carnations, marigolds, elderflowers, broom flowers and nasturtiums all make excellent vinegars. In Elizabethan days, the preserved flowers themselves were also served in winter salads.

Rose Petal Vinegar

Rose petal vinegar is said to ease headaches caused by hot sun. It looks pretty and adds the beautiful summery flavour of roses to a salad. Use the petals of the dark-red, old-fashioned damask rose if possible. Pack the petals into the measuring jug.

Metric	US	Imperial	
600ml	2½ cups	1 pint	unsprayed garden rose petals
600ml	2½ cups	1 pint	white wine vinegar
50g	¼ cup	2oz	caster sugar (optional)

Wipe the rose petals carefully and remove the white heel from each. Place the petals in a large jar. Put the vinegar and sugar in a saucepan and heat gently until the sugar has dissolved. Leave to cool, then pour over the rose petals, making sure that they are completely covered. Cover and leave the jar in the sun to help draw out the flavour for 3–4 weeks. Strain and pour into sterilised bottles. Cork and use as required.

Elderflower Vinegar

This is particularly good for marinades and salad dressings. Gather the flowers on a dry day just as they begin to open.

Metric	US	Imperial	
			about 7 elderflower heads
600ml	2½ cups	1 pint	white wine vinegar

Pull off the flowers from the elderflower heads using a fork. Discard the stalks and leave the blossoms overnight on paper to dry. Place them in the vinegar, cover and leave the jar in the sun for 3–4 weeks before straining, bottling and corking.

Fruit Vinegars

Fruit vinegars are excellent in salad dressings. They provide useful substitutes for wine or other alcohol when deglazing a frying or roasting pan to make sauce or gravy, particularly to accompany game. Try pouring fruit vinegars over grilled meat, or combining them with melted butter for fish.

Raspberry Vinegar

This very traditional product of the fruit garden has enjoyed vogue status in recent years. It is highly rated by chefs and food enthusiasts for its remarkable fresh and fruity fragrance. You will need fresh or frozen raspberries to start the recipe and the same quantity again to complete it a week later. Raspberry vinegar is wonderful on a salad of bitter leaves.

Metric	US	Imperial	
900g	2lb	2lb	fresh or frozen raspberries
600ml	2½ cups	1 pint	red wine vinegar

Lay half the raspberries in a bowl or plastic container and cover with the vinegar. Cover with a cloth and leave to stand for 5-7 days in a warm place, stirring occasionally. Strain off the liquid, then repeat again with the remaining raspberries. Strain through a jelly bag into sterilised bottles, adding a few whole berries if you wish. Seal and store for no less than 1 month to mature before using. For a refreshing drink, add 15ml/1tbsp/1tbsp of raspberry vinegar to a glass of iced water.

Lemon Vinegar

This is particularly good in salad dressings and mayonnaise instead of wine vinegar, especially when they are being served with fish or chicken.

Metric	US	Imperial	
2	2	2	large lemons
600ml	2½ cups	1 pint	white wine vinegar
3	3	3	small sprigs lemon balm

Wash and dry the lemons. Peel the rind very thinly without removing any pith. Cut the lemons and squeeze the juice into a sterilised bottle, adding the lemon peel. Top up the bottle with vinegar. Wash the lemon balm, dry, and add to the vinegar. Cork the bottle and shake well. Leave in a cool place to stand for at least 3 weeks. Strain the lemon vinegar through muslin, pour back into the bottle. Cover and store in a cool place. Use as required.

VARIATION

Orange Vinegar Substitute 2 medium-sized oranges for the lemons and omit the lemon balm. Make as above. Add 1 or 2 strips of freshly pared orange rind to the bottle before covering and storing.

Spiced Blackberry Vinegar

This is good in marinades and sauces especially for duck or goose.

Metric	US	Imperial	
450g	1lb	1lb	blackberries
1	1	1	cinnamon stick
5ml	1tsp	1tsp	allspice berries
5ml	1tsp	1tsp	whole cloves
300ml	1¼ cups	½ pint	white wine vinegar
			a few fresh blackberries to finish

Pick over the berries and remove any mouldy or damaged parts. Break the cinnamon stick into pieces, then tie all the spices in a piece of muslin.

Put the vinegar into a pan with the bag of spices and bring to the boil. Lower the heat and simmer for 5 minutes. Add the blackberries and simmer for a further 10 minutes. Remove from the heat and leave to cool completely. Discard the spice bag.

Strain the vinegar through a double layer of muslin into a sterilised bottle. Add a few fresh blackberries to give an attractive finish. Cover the bottle and use as required.

Blueberry and Basil Vinegar

Excellent for salad dressings and sauces, this vinegar is a particularly beautiful colour.

Metric	US	Imperial	
			a small bunch of fresh basil
225g	8oz	8oz	fresh blueberries
600ml	2½ cups	1 pint	white wine vinegar
7·5ml	1½ tsp	1½ tsp	fresh chives, chopped
			a fresh chive flower, and a few blueberries to finish

Strip the basil leaves from their stalks. Tear into small pieces and discard the stalks. Put the blueberries and a little vinegar into a china or glass bowl and crush them with the back of a wooden spoon to release their juices. Stir in the remaining vinegar with the basil and the chives. Pour the mixture into a large sterilised jar, cover and shake well. Keep in a cool dark place for 4 weeks, shaking the jar from time to time.

Strain through a double layer of muslin into a sterilised bottle. Add a chive flower and a few blueberries to the bottle to give an attractive finish. Cover and use as required.

Orange-Scented Vinegar

Use in salad dressings, sauces and marinades.

Metric	US	Imperial	
2	2	2	small oranges
600ml	2½ cups	1 pint	white wine vinegar
			freshly pared orange rind to finish

Thinly pare the rind from the oranges with a potato peeler, without taking off the pith. Cut the oranges in half and squeeze out the juice. Put the orange rind and juice into a sterilised jar, then pour on the vinegar. Seal the jar and shake well. Keep in a cool dark place for at least 3 weeks to allow the flavour to develop, then strain through muslin into a sterilised bottle.

Add 1 or 2 strips of freshly pared orange rind to the bottle. Seal and store in a cool place. Use as required.

Spiced Vinegars

Pickling Vinegar

This spiced vinegar is used in a large number of pickles and chutneys. It must be made at least 6 weeks before you intend using it, as the spices need to steep in the vinegar for maximum flavour. Whole spices give a better result.

Metric	US	Imperial	
15ml	1 tbsp	1 tbsp	celery seeds
15ml	1 tbsp	1 tbsp	mustard seeds
15ml	1 tbsp	1 tbsp	green cardamom pods, bruised
10ml	2 tsp	2 tsp	coriander seeds
10ml	2 tsp	2 tsp	whole cloves
10ml	2 tsp	2 tsp	allspice berries
10	10	10	dried red chillies
15ml	1 tbsp	1 tbsp	black peppercorns, lightly crushed
25g	1 oz	1 oz	fresh root ginger, peeled and finely sliced
1·2 litres	5 cups	2 pints	cider, malt or white wine vinegar

Mix all the spices together in a bowl, then divide them between two, clean, dry bottles and fill to the top with vinegar. Cover and leave to stand for 1–2 months, shaking occasionally. Strain the vinegar before using.

Quick Pickling Vinegar
This method is useful if you need the vinegar quickly. Use the same recipe as before, but put all the ingredients into a bowl. Cover with a plate and stand the bowl over a saucepan of water. Bring the water to the boil, remove the pan from the heat and leave the bowl over the pan for up to 2 hours to allow the spices to steep in the warm vinegar. Strain and use within a short time.

Sweet Pickling Vinegar

This vinegar is ideal for sweet pickles and fruit pickles. Any vinegar can be used, but use white sugar with white vinegar.

Metric	US	Imperial	
900g	4¼ cups	2 lb	brown or white sugar
1·2 litres	5 cups	2 pints	white distilled, white wine or malt vinegar
15 ml	1 tbsp	1 tbsp	whole cloves
1	1	1	cinnamon stick
15 ml	1 tbsp	1 tbsp	coriander seeds
15 ml	1 tbsp	1 tbsp	whole allspice berries
6	6	6	blades of mace

Dissolve the sugar in the vinegar and pour into a large jar or bottle. Put the spices in a muslin bag and add to the vinegar. Leave to steep for 6–8 weeks, tightly covered. Strain and use as required.

Chilli Vinegar

This is best made with hot red chillies. It adds fire to sauces and dressings, or spices up marinades and casseroles.

Metric	US	Imperial	
			about 20 red fresh chillies, halved and seeded
7·5 ml	½ tbsp	½ tbsp	mustard seeds, lightly crushed
600 ml	2½ cups	1 pint	cider vinegar

Put the vinegar in a pan and bring to the boil. Add the chillies and mustard seeds, then bring back to the boil. Cover and remove from the heat. Leave until cold, then pour into a sterilised jar. Cover and leave for 5–6 weeks. Strain the vinegar through muslin into a sterilised bottle. It is now ready to use.

Flavoured Oils

Infusing oils with a single flavour or a compatible combination of herbs and spices is a lovely way to make personalised gifts for friends. They are simple to make and far cheaper than bought.

Almost any herb or spice can be used, along with aromatic fruits, such as lemons, oranges or limes. Aromatic oils can be used in salad dressings and marinades, for browning meat and vegetables, grilling, roasting vegetables and stir-frying – in fact for any dish where you would use an unflavoured oil. Simply make sure that the taste of the flavoured oil complements the ingredients you are using.

Choosing the oil

There is such a wide choice today, each with a special flavour of its own. Light oils, such as sunflower, rapeseed or corn, do not dominate the taste of the added ingredients, so are generally suitable for infusing with the more pungent herbs and spices. Luxury oils, such as peanut, sesame, walnut and hazelnut, have their own distinctive tastes. Use these in small quantities: not only are they expensive but soon go rancid. The best of all oils for flavouring is olive.

Selecting the flavourings

1 If you are using herbs, they should be freshly picked and lightly dried on kitchen paper to remove excess moisture, then bruised lightly to release their aromas. (Put the herbs on a chopping board and place a large chef's knife on top of them. Using the palm of your hand, press down firmly on the flat of the knife.)
2 Dried spices, such as peppercorns and chillies, should be as fresh as possible and should be lightly bruised in a pestle and mortar to release their flavour.
3 Fresh ingredients, such as lemon grass, ginger and garlic should also be as fresh as possible and again, lightly bruised with the flat side of a chef's knife.

Making up the oil

Insert the prepared flavourings into sterilised bottles, then pour in the oil to within 3mm/$\frac{1}{8}$in of the top, making sure that all the ingredients are completely covered so that mould cannot grow. Seal the bottles. Leave for about 2 weeks in a cool, dark place, shaking from time to time. During this time the flavour will develop, so taste the oil occasionally to see when it is ready to use.

Straining the oil

If you prefer the flavour not to get any stronger at this stage, or if you want the oil to last longer, especially if it contains fresh ingredients, strain through a double layer of muslin into freshly sterilised bottles. (Add a fresh herb sprig if you wish, for decoration and identification.)

Sealing and Storage

Seal the bottle tightly with a non-corrosive, screw-top lid, then label clearly and keep in the fridge for 3–4 months. (If you are using a recycled bottle, the oil must be kept in the fridge because the seal will not be as tight.) The storage time will depend on the flavouring ingredients. Those that contain fresh ingredients, such as herbs, garlic or fruit, unless strained first, will only last about 3 months. Oils that have been infused with dry ingredients will keep about 6 months.

Hazelnut Oil with Dill and Peppercorns

This is excellent for frying and grilling fish.

Metric	US	Imperial	
15g	1/2 oz	1/2 oz	fresh dill, lightly bruised
5ml	1 tsp	1 tsp	mixed peppercorns, lightly crushed
300ml	1 1/4 cups	1/2 pint	hazelnut oil

Pack the dill into a sterilised bottle with the peppercorns. Pour in the oil, cover and shake well. Keep for 2 weeks before using.

Lemon-flavoured Olive Oil

This is excellent as a dressing for a green salad when mixed with a squeeze of lemon juice and a little sea salt. It is good dribbled over a baguette before being topped with goat's cheese and browned under the grill.

Metric	US	Imperial	
3	3	3	lemons (preferably organic)
600ml	2 1/2 cups	1 pint	virgin olive oil

Scrub the lemons and dry them well. Remove the rind using a lemon zester or grater, avoiding all the pith. Put in a sterilised bottle and pour in the oil. Cover and shake well. Leave for 1 week before using.

Mixed Herb and Garlic Oil

This is excellent for grilling and barbecuing. Experiment with other combinations of herbs and spices.

Metric	US	Imperial	
2	2	2	sprigs of fresh rosemary
2	2	2	sprigs of fresh marjoram or oregano
2	2	2	sprigs of fresh thyme
2	2	2	garlic cloves, peeled
2	2	2	bay leaves
6	6	6	black peppercorns, lightly crushed
1	1	1	small dried red chilli
300ml	1¼ cups	½ pint	extra virgin or virgin olive oil

Lightly bruise the herbs and garlic to release their aroma. Place all the ingredients, including the chilli, in a sterilised bottle, pouring in the oil last. Cover and shake well. Keep for 2 weeks before using.

Sissinghurst's Flavoured Oils

The chef at Sissinghurst prepares a number of flavoured oils for the restaurant. Here are several of his suggested combinations, but do experiment with your own. Make in the usual way (see page 50).

Chilli, Garlic and Marjoram Oil
Add 8 peeled garlic cloves, 1 fresh red chilli and a small bunch of fresh marjoram to 1 litre/4½ cups/1¾ pints olive or sunflower oil.

Lemon and Thyme Oil
Add the peel of 2 lemons (without pith), 8 sprigs fresh thyme, 4 peeled garlic cloves and 12 black peppercorns to 1 litre/4½ cups/1¾ pints virgin olive or sunflower oil.

Garlic Olive Oil
This is dribbled on grilled vegetables, fish, poultry and meat, or on pizzas. Use instead of butter on pasta or to intensify the flavour of any pasta sauce. It is also delicious added to mashed potatoes instead of butter. To make a quick garlic bread, simply dribble on fresh, hot crusty bread. Add peeled, lightly bruised garlic cloves to extra virgin olive oil – make it to your own taste. Leave to infuse for 2 weeks.

Basil, Sage and Peppercorn Oil
Add 4 fresh sage leaves, 6 sprigs of fresh basil and 12 black peppercorns to 1 litre/ 4½ cups/1¾ pints virgin olive or sunflower oil.

Lime, Garlic and Sesame Seed Oil
Add the zest of 1 lime (avoiding the pith), 1 peeled garlic clove and 7·5ml/½ tbsp/ ½ tbsp sesame seeds to 300ml/1¼ cups/½ pint sesame oil.

Chilli and Orange Oil
Add 4 fresh red chillies, 1 bay leaf and 1 large piece of orange peel to 600ml/ 2½ cups/1 pint olive or sunflower oil.

Thai Basting Oil

Metric	US	Imperial	
2	2	2	pieces of lemon grass
2·5cm	1in	1in	piece of fresh root ginger
3	3	3	sprigs of fresh coriander
2	2	2	lime leaves
2	2	2	dried red chillies
300ml	1¼ cups	½ pint	peanut oil

Lightly bruise the lemon grass, ginger and coriander, then place in a sterilised bottle with the lime leaves and chillies. Pour in the oil, cover and shake well. Store for 2 weeks before using.

Preserves in Oil

Not only can oil be flavoured with herbs and spices, but it can also be used as a preserving medium. Foods preserved in oil make unusual gifts when packed in attractive jars with fresh herbs and spices. The choice of oil will depend on how strong you want the flavour to be. Ordinary olive oil is much milder in flavour than extra virgin, but both are wonderful as preservers of foods. Sunflower or corn oil can be used if a neutral-flavoured oil is required. Nut oils tend to go rancid much more quickly so avoid using these. Serve with salads, as accompaniments or appetisers. The leftover flavoured oil can be used for cooking and in salad dressings and marinades.

Goat's Cheeses with Herbs in Oil

Leave the cheeses for 2-3 weeks before using, to allow the oil to take on the flavour of the cheese and vice versa. Use in salads or on crispbread.

Metric	US	Imperial	
4	4	4	small round goat's cheeses, each weighing about 75g/3oz/3oz
6	6	6	sprigs of fresh thyme
6	6	6	bay leaves
12	12	12	black peppercorns, lightly crushed
			extra virgin olive oil

Cut each goat's cheese into quarters and pack into a sterilised jar, layering with the herbs and peppercorns as you go. Pour in the olive oil to cover the cheese by 1·25cm/ ½in. Cover and keep in the refrigerator for 2-3 weeks before using to allow the flavours to develop.

Chilli Lemon Slices in Olive Oil

Limes can be used instead of lemons if you wish.

Metric	US	Imperial	
675g	1½lb	1½lb	lemons, preferably organic
125g	¾ cup	4oz	sea salt
2	2	2	dried red chillies
2	2	2	bay leaves
18·75ml	1¼ tbsp	1¼ tbsp	paprika
5ml	1 tsp	1 tsp	chilli powder
300ml	1¼ cups	½ pint	virgin olive oil

Wash and cut the lemons into slices about 5mm/¼in thick. Discard all the pips from the slices, then arrange them in a single layer in one or two shallow china or glass dishes. Sprinkle with the salt, cover with a clean cloth and leave to stand for 24 hours. This draws out excess moisture from the lemons.

Drain the lemon slices, leaving the salt on the surface and set aside. Roughly chop the chillies and crumble the bay leaves into small pieces. Mix them in a small bowl with the paprika and chilli powder. Carefully pack the salt-encrusted lemon slices into dry sterilised jars, sprinkling the spice mixture evenly between the layers.

Pour in the oil almost to the top of the jars, making sure that the lemons are covered by 1·25cm/½in. Cover the jars and keep in a cool dark place for at least 1 week before using, to allow the flavours to develop.

Mushrooms in Garlic Oil

Choose firm, very fresh button mushrooms for this recipe.

Metric	US	Imperial	
350g	12oz	12oz	button mushrooms
300ml	1¼ cups	½ pint	extra virgin olive oil
			juice of 2 lemons
6	6	6	black peppercorns, lightly crushed
2	2	2	garlic cloves, peeled
2	2	2	bay leaves

Wipe the mushrooms with kitchen paper, then trim the stalks level with the caps. Place them in a china or glass bowl with half the oil and the other ingredients. Stir well and leave to stand, covered with a clean cloth, for 3–4 hours.

Pour the mushroom mixture into a saucepan and bring to the boil. Simmer, stirring from time to time, for 15 minutes, then remove from the heat and leave to cool.

Drain the mushrooms through a nylon sieve and pat dry with kitchen paper. Pack them into sterilised jars and pour in the remaining oil to cover the mushrooms by 1·25cm/½in. Seal the jars. Store in a fridge and use within two weeks.

Home-dried Tomatoes in Olive Oil

This is a way of preserving tomatoes you have dried at home (see page 60). They are delicious when freshly made, but are even better after 2 weeks, when the flavour has developed.

dried tomatoes
bay leaves
extra virgin olive oil

Pack the dried tomatoes into clean sterilised jars tucking in a few bay leaves. Pour in the oil to cover the tomatoes by 1·25cm/½in. Cover the jars and keep in a cool dark place for at least 2 weeks before using. They will keep for 6 months.

Roasted Sweet Peppers in Oil

Peppers can be bought all the year round, but are at their best late summer and autumn, the season when they naturally mature. Red peppers have the best flavour for this recipe, but orange and yellow peppers can be treated in the same way. The roasting brings out their sweetness and gives them a full, rich flavour. Serve as an instant salad or appetiser; use instead of a sauce; or add to pasta dishes. The pepper-flavoured oil can be used for cooking and in salad dressings.

Metric	US	Imperial	
2-3	2-3	2-3	red peppers
2-3	2-3	2-3	plump garlic cloves, peeled and lightly bruised
			a few sprigs of fresh marjoram or oregano
			extra virgin olive oil

To roast the peppers, place them on a baking tray and cook in a hot oven 425°F/ 210°C/gas mark 7 for about 30 minutes, or until the skins start to blister and the peppers start to feel soft. (Do not leave them too long or the flesh will become very soft.) Leave until cool enough to handle, then remove the skin.

Cut the peppers in half on a plate to retain the juices. Discard the stems and seeds. Cut into thick slices, then layer in a sterilised jar with the garlic cloves and herb sprigs. Pour in the reserved juices and enough oil to cover the peppers by 1·25cm/½in.

Cover and store in the refrigerator. Use within 2 weeks. Because of the high moisture content of most commercial peppers, they do not keep long. If you grow your own, they will keep for about 2 months

CHAPTER 4

Dried Fruit, Vegetables, Herbs and Flowers

Drying is the oldest and most natural way of preserving food. The early inhabitants of Britain probably ate wild berries and fruit where they were found, but when people started carrying produce home, they had the problem of preserving some of it. They may have solved this by leaving food outside in the sun to dry naturally or by hanging it up near a fire. Both these ancient methods relied on the slow removal of all moisture and this is still the main rule for successful drying. If the moisture is not removed slowly, the resulting food is tough and wrinkled, and no amount of soaking and careful cooking will improve it.

The drying process is very simple. Fruit, vegetables, nuts, herbs and flowers all contain a large amount of water; if this is evaporated, enzyme activity and the growth of micro-organisms, which cause the food to deteriorate and rot, is stopped. Drying can be carried out at home with very little special equipment and it is extremely rewarding. If the sun is hot enough, you can dry produce in the open air over 4–5 days, but in Britain this method can be a little unreliable! A very good result can be achieved by drying in a cool oven, in an airing cupboard, over a boiler or radiator, or in a place which provides dry, constant heat. Ensure there is adequate ventilation to allow the moisture from the produce to escape and that the food is protected from dust.

Gas, electric or solid-fuel ovens can all be used for drying, provided that the oven can be set to a very low temperature. If the temperature is too hot, the produce will cook and the skins will split; if it is not hot enough, the produce will rot. Gas is perhaps the least satisfactory, as the heat has to be below that of the lowest regulo setting; that is, on the lowest flame possible.

Propping open the oven door lowers the temperature and provides the required ventilation. With electric ovens, the temperature for drying should be between 50–70°C/110–150°F, but check it occasionally during the drying process. Drying can be carried out either as a continuous process or intermittently over several days; this should not affect the quality of the finished product. If you are using a solid-fuel cooker, place the produce to be dried in the 'simmering oven' and leave the door ajar.

Spread the fruit or vegetables in a single layer on wire or wooden racks (cooling racks are ideal) covered with scalded muslin or cheesecloth. The cloth must be scalded before use, even if it is new, to stop it scorching and also to prevent the produce from absorbing any odours or flavours from the cloth. Once dried, the food will keep for many months if the drying process has been carried out completely and correctly.

Dried Fruit

Fruits are easier to dry than vegetables because their higher sugar content assists with preservation. As with any method of preservation, it is very important to use high quality, fresh, ripe fruit which will retain a good colour and flavour. Most fruit requires 4-6 hours continuous drying at 50-70°C/110-150°F. Do not allow the temperature to rise above this level for at least the first hour, as this will cause the surface of the fruit to harden, prolonging the process of evaporation and possibly causing the skins of plums, apricots and peaches to burst.

When the drying process is completed, remove the trays from the heat and leave the fruit to cool at room temperature for at least 12 hours. Finally, check that each fruit is thoroughly dry before storing – a small patch of moisture will turn the whole batch bad. Pack the fruit in containers lined with greaseproof paper: wooden or cardboard boxes or biscuit tins may be used. Store in a very dry, well-ventilated place away from strong light.

Dried fruit can be eaten as it is, as a snack or sweetmeat, or it can be soaked for 24 hours in lukewarm water or wine, using the soaking liquor for cooking and adding any chosen spices, flavourings and sugar as required. The most suitable fruits for drying are apples, pears, plums, apricots, peaches, nectarines, figs, grapes and bananas. Most small fruits and berries tend to lose their shape.

Dried Apple Rings

Choose firm, ripe, but not over-ripe, eating or cooking apples. Wash, peel and core them using a silver or stainless steel knife. Slice into rings 6mm/¼in thick and drop immediately into a bowl of lightly salted water – 1 × 5ml/1 tsp/1 tsp salt to 1·2 litres/ 5 cups/2 pints water – to prevent discoloration and leave for 10 minutes. Drain, shaking off excess water, and pat them dry with a clean tea-towel or cloth. Spread them, with edges slightly overlapping, on wire racks covered with cheesecloth or muslin, or thread on bamboo canes or wooden dowelling, which can rest on the runners of the oven. Place in a cold oven and heat gently to about 50°C/110°F. Then open the oven door and allow the temperature to rise to 70°C/150°F. If the drying process is continuous, the apple rings will need 4-6 hours. Test by squeezing: if no water comes out, the fruit is done. The finished texture should be a little like chamois leather, pliable but not brittle, and the colour should be dark cream. Cool as quickly as possible to prevent shrivelling, pack and store as suggested above.

VARIATIONS

Apple or Pear Quarters Peel, core and quarter the fruit after washing and drying them on a tea-towel. Dry as above.

Chopped-up dried apple can be used with currants, raisins and sultanas to make them go further in cakes or puddings.

Crab Apples These can be dried whole, which was the original way of drying apples. Wash, dry and core the apples, then thread on to wooden sticks or thick string and dry as above.

Dried Apricots, Peaches, Nectarines or Plums

Use ripe but firm fruit, selecting large apricots or plums. Halve and stone them or leave them whole. Spread on trays or racks, covered with cheesecloth or muslin, with the cut sides uppermost to retain the juice. Dry slowly at a temperature of 60°C/120°F until the skins start to shrivel, then increase the temperature to 70°C/150°F. Squeeze the fruit between the fingers to check if it has dried: if the skin does not break and no juice oozes out, the fruit is sufficiently dry. This will take 16–24 hours of continuous drying – much longer than for apples and pears. Cool, pack and store.

VARIATION
Damsons or cherries Dry these whole, as for apricots above.

Dried Vegetables

Vegetables for drying must be young and fresh. Dry slowly at the same temperatures as for fruit and leave the dried vegetables to cool for several hours or overnight before storing in containers lined with greaseproof paper or in tightly corked jars kept away from the light.

Dried Mushrooms

Any edible fungi will dry well. It is a very good way of coping with a glut. When your freezer is full of them and your family are sick of mushroom soup, drying is the answer. Once mushrooms are dried, they take up very little storage space as they lose a large amount of water.

Mushrooms must be very fresh. Wipe them over with a damp cloth, or peel them if they are very dirty. Spread on trays or racks without overlapping, or thread on strings, knotting the string between each mushroom so that they do not touch. Place the trays in the oven at a temperature of 50°C/110°F, propping the door ajar to allow good ventilation. If you are drying on strings, hang them in the airing cupboard or in a dry, warm place. Leave to dry until crisp to the touch. This will take from 6–12 hours. Cool and store in airtight containers until required.

Dried mushrooms can be added without soaking to soups, stews, sauces and casseroles. To fry them or to use in omelettes, soak them for about 1 hour in tepid water or milk, then pat dry before cooking.

Mushroom Powder This makes a very welcome addition to the store cupboard. It adds flavour to gravies, soups, stews, casseroles, dumplings and stuffings. Dry the mushrooms as above until they feel crisp, Crush to a powder using a pestle and mortar, or simply crumble them between your fingers. Store in an airtight jar. Add 5ml/1tsp/1tsp mushroom powder to soups, casseroles, stews, gravies or sauces towards the end of their cooking time.

Dried Tomatoes

Home-grown tomatoes are ideal for this recipe as they usually have a good flavour. Otherwise, buy tomatoes in the summer when they have the best flavour and are at their cheapest. They should be ripe but firm.

Metric	US	Imperial	
1·35kg	3lb	3lb	medium-sized tomatoes
2·5–5ml	½–1tsp	½–1tsp	sea salt

Cut the tomatoes in half horizontally and scoop out all the pulp including the seeds and central pith (use this to make soup or a sauce). Arrange the tomato cases cut sides up and sprinkle very lightly with salt.

Turn them cut sides down on a wire rack, close together but not touching. Put the rack on a shelf in a very low oven 60-80°C/150-175°F, placing a sheet of foil on the bottom of the oven to catch the drips. Prop the door open with a skewer. This will allow the tomatoes to dry rather than cook. If they seem to be cooking, reduce the temperature slightly or lower the shelf if the bottom part of your oven is cooler than the top.

The tomatoes will take 8-12 hours to dry depending on your oven, but check them from time to time. They will shrivel to half their size and are ready when nearly all the moisture has evaporated but they are still soft and pliable.

When they are sufficiently dry, remove from the oven and leave to cool on the rack. Use immediately, freeze or preserve in olive oil (see page 55).

Dried Herbs and Flowers

Housewives have traditionally hung bunches of dried herbs and flowers in the kitchen for winter use and large quantities were strewn on floors to pervade the house with their sweet smell and deter vermin. A wide range of herbs and flowers were grown in garden plots. Thomas Tusser, an East Anglian farmer, compiled in 1590 a list of 'herbs necessary for the kitchen garden' giving over one hundred, many of which are rarely heard of in cookery today and look very strange to modern eyes. The herb gardens created at Buckland Abbey in Devon and Hardwick Hall in Derbyshire are planted predominantly with herbs that would have been familiar to a sixteenth-century household. The Elizabethans delighted in coloured foods: purple violets and blue borage flowers would have made a striking contrast with red mints, nettles and fennel, pale-coloured buds of primroses and alexanders and a variety of green leaves.

In the seventeenth century, the aromatic herbs of Mediterranean origin, described as 'sweet' or 'fine' herbs, were in favour. French cuisine had considerable influence on English cookery at this time, especially after the Restoration of Charles II in 1660. This interest in herbs continued until the end of the nineteenth century; it is only in the twentieth century that interest and knowledge waned. However, in the past few years we have shown renewed interest in experimenting with herbs and flowers in our cooking and many people are now growing their own. Even if you do not have a garden, herbs can be grown successfully in window boxes.

To Dry Herbs

Drying herbs is a simple and rewarding task. Herbs are at their most pungent just before flowering and this is the best time to pick them for preserving. Choose a dry day and harvest the herbs early in the morning after the dew has dried and before the sun is fully on them.

Line a shelf in the airing cupboard with muslin, or lay a piece of muslin on a large, wire rack and place it on top of the boiler. Lay the herbs on the muslin, spacing them apart, cover with a second piece of muslin and leave for 1–4 days until dry and brittle. Do not leave longer than necessary as they will lose their flavour. Crumble the leaves, or strip them from the stems and store in clean, glass jars in a cool, dark cupboard.

Using Dried Herbs

Dried herbs do not retain their flavour and aroma for long, so ideally they should be used up within 6 months. When you use dried herbs remember that, because of dehydration, they are much more concentrated than fresh herbs – roughly three times as strong.

The best herbs for drying are bay, fennel, marjoram, dill, sage, oregano, thyme, coriander, savory and tarragon. Rosemary can be dried, but the leaves become needle-like and must be tied in a muslin bag for cooking. Parsley, chives, mint and basil can also be dried, but are not very successful, so are better used fresh.

Mixed Herbs

It is well worth making up your own mixed herbs. Crumble up equal quantities of, say, thyme, marjoram, savory and parsley. Mix together and pack into airtight jars or bottles.

Herbes de Provence

In Provence dried herbs are sold in little terracotta pots topped with the local patterned cloth, or in brightly coloured bags of the same material. By a simple blending of five herbs, you can make your own blend for Provençal dishes.

Crumble equal quantities of dried oregano, thyme, savory, marjoram and rosemary. Mix together well, then pack into airtight jars.

Italian Seasoning

Use 8-12 dried bay leaves (depending on size), 30ml/2tbsp/2tbsp each of dried thyme, oregano and sage, and 30ml/2tbsp/2tbsp each of freshly ground black pepper and paprika. Crush the bay leaves with a rolling pin until they are broken into quite fine pieces. Alternatively, use a pestle and mortar. Mix them with all the remaining ingredients until thoroughly combined, then pack into a clean airtight jar. The herbs are now ready for use.

Sweet Herb Powder

Thyme, marjoram and sage are known as 'sweet herbs'. Crush the dried herbs to a powder between your fingers, then mix and place in airtight containers. This powder is particularly useful for flavouring stocks and stuffings.

Faggot of Sweet Herbs

This is the original name for the modern 'bouquet garni' which was introduced into English cookery through the influence of French cuisine in the seventeenth century. It was traditionally a small bundle of mixed herbs cooked with a stew or other dish and removed before serving. It usually consists of sprigs of thyme, marjoram, parsley and a bay leaf, but you can use dried mixed herbs or add other herbs and spices to give different flavours for different dishes. Most soup and casseroles are improved by the addition of a 'faggot' or 'bouquet garni'.

---

1 small dried bay leaf
generous pinch of mixed herbs
pinch of dried parsley
6 black peppercorns, lightly crushed
1 whole clove

Cut a small square of clean muslin or cheesecloth. Place herbs and spices in the centre. Tie into a small bag with fine string or cotton, leaving a long end of cotton free to tie the bouquet garni to the handle of the casserole or pan. This way, it can be retrieved easily before serving, instead of the cook searching without success and some poor guest chewing unhappily on an unidentified little parcel!

VARIATIONS

Chicken Bouquet Garni Fill a muslin bag with a generous pinch of dried parsley and dried marjoram, hyssop, savory and ground nutmeg. Add to casseroles, soups and sauces, especially with chicken, duck, pork or lamb.

Fish Bouquet Garni Fill a muslin bag with a pinch of dill seeds and dried tarragon, 6 white peppercorns lightly crushed and a pinch of fennel seeds. Add to fish or even pork dishes.

Vegetable Bouquet Garni Fill a muslin bag with a generous pinch of dried parsley and dried mint, dill seeds and dried basil. Use in vegetable casseroles and sauces to accompany vegetables.

Beef Bouquet Garni This flavoured bouquet garni gives a spicy taste to all red meat casseroles and stews. Fill a muslin bag with a generous pinch of dried thyme, 1 bay leaf, 6 juniper berries lightly crushed and 3 whole cloves. This is excellent for venison casseroles.

Faggot of Herbs Wrapped in a Leek Wrap a small sprig of dried thyme, marjoram, parsley and a bay leaf in a 15cm/6in piece of leek (the green folded part). Secure with cotton or fine string and use to flavour soups and casseroles.

Herbal Teas

Teas made of dried aromatic leaves, flowers, seeds or roots steeped in water are ancient and popular drinks. If you are not used to herb teas, try mint, rose-hip, peppermint, lemon verbena and lemon thyme first, as they are all easy to enjoy.

Put the leaves or flowers into a warm teapot, pour boiling water over and leave to infuse for 3–5 minutes depending on the herb. Allow 5ml/1tsp/1tsp dried herbs or 15ml/1tbsp/1tbsp fresh for each cup of boiling water.

Seeds and roots are usually ground in a pestle and mortar just before use. Then 15ml/1tbsp/1tbsp is added to 2 cups of boiling water and simmered until the water is reduced by half.

To Dry Seeds

Seeds such as coriander, dill, fennel and caraway can also be dried at home. These should be picked as soon as they have formed on the plants.

Pick the seed head and lay the stems on trays lined with kitchen paper. Cover with more kitchen paper to keep off dust. Leave in a dry, warm, airy place for 10-14 days until the seeds are dry. Shake the seeds from the flower heads on to the paper, then pack in clean, dry jars. Alternatively, tie the stems in bunches and place them, heads down, in paper bags (not plastic). Tie the bags in place and hang until dry. Shake the seeds out into the bag, then pack in jars and store as for herbs.

To Dry Flowers

Many flowers can be dried for culinary use or for making herbal teas. Not all flowers are edible, so do not experiment without seeking expert advice.

The following are some common flowers that are useful to dry for later use: rosemary, thyme, lavender, borage, chive, chamomile, lime, violets, primroses, rose petals, elder and pot marigold.

Gather the flowers when they are in full bloom on a dry, sunny day after the dew has dried. Check that they are insect-free and discard any that are badly infected. Never wash the flowers as this will remove much of the fragrance. Remove all stems, leaves and greenery. Cut away the white or pale-green heels at the base of rose and marigold petals. Small flowers and buds may be left whole. Spread the flowers or petals on large racks, trays or baskets and dry in a well-ventilated place away from the sun; the airing cupboard is ideal. Shake or stir them around with your hands several times a day until they are completely dry and brittle to the touch. If they are even slightly damp, they will spoil during storage. Pack in cardboard boxes or airtight tins – biscuit tins are ideal – and store in a dry place.

Mint, Chamomile, Peppermint and Linden
The flowers of these herbs can be dried whole and the dried flower heads used to make delicious teas (see page 63).

Fruit curds, cheeses and pastes: Apple and Lemon Curds, Quince Cheese and Quince Pastes. (*NTPL/Andreas von Einsiedel*)

Dried Pot Marigold

The marigold is a prolific garden plant and flowers from April to late autumn, so it is easy to obtain plenty of petals. Marigolds are dried in the usual way, but only the petals are used, both for colouring and flavour. They have been used in cooking since the Middle Ages when they were added with other flowers, such as dandelions, daisies and herbs, to 'pottage', a kind of thick soup. Use a good pinch of petals to add flavour, colour and spice to soups, casseroles, stews and stuffings.

The Elizabethans used marigolds as a vegetable dye to colour cheese and butter, and if a little boiling water is poured on to a few petals the resulting liquid can be used to colour and flavour rice instead of turmeric or saffron. In fact, pot marigold was once known as 'the poor man's saffron'. Petals can also be included in bread and cake mixtures and they make a beautiful tea.

Broth Posies

These are very useful to have in your store cupboard for flavouring soups and casseroles. Make up several at a time.

Pinch of dried marigold flowers
Pinch of dried parsley
Pinch of dried thyme
1 bay leaf

Wrap the herbs in a small square of muslin. Secure with cotton or fine string and store in an airtight jar.

Dried Elderflowers

The elder has sweet-smelling flowers which probably have more uses than any other single species of blossom. They are so cool and refreshing just eaten straight from the branch. If you want to dry them, cut the flower clusters whole and check that they are free from insects – don't wash them. Dry as for other flowers. Use the dried blossoms to make drinks and wine or flavour ice-creams and other creamy puddings. They can also be used to flavour any dish made with gooseberries, including sauces, jams, jellies and chutneys.

Quinces growing in the walled garden at Berrington Hall in Herefordshire. (*NTPL/Stephen Robson*)

CHAPTER 5

Flavoured Sugars, Salts and Syrups

Of all the items on the medieval spice account, sugar was the one destined to have the greatest effect on Britain's eating habits. The Romans had known it only as a medicine, but now it came into its own in the kitchen. As well as plain sugars of several grades, rose- and violet-flavoured sugars were imported, and those who could afford them consumed large quantities. Apparently, in 1287 the royal household used 677lb of sugar, 300lb of violet sugar and 1,900lb of rose sugar.

Flavoured sugars are a delightful addition to the modern store cupboard and are so simple to make. Use them to flavour plain puddings, custards, milk puddings, biscuits and cakes. It is well worth experimenting with different herbs, flowers and flavourings.

Herb Sugars

Herbs recommended for perfuming sugar include angelica, bay, aniseed, blackcurrant leaves, rose geranium, and other scented leaf geraniums, hyssop, lavender, lemon balm, lemon verbena, mint (especially eau-de-cologne and pineapple), rose petals, rosemary, elderflowers, sweet cicely and sweet violet.

Lavender Sugar

Hidcote Manor Garden Restaurant uses lavender sugar in a number of their dishes to celebrate the famous Hidcote Lavender. It is delicious in any milk or creamy pudding, sprinkled on biscuits and cakes after cooking, used with butter for glazing carrots and added to old-fashioned cakes and puddings made from carrots.

Metric	US	Imperial	
50g	2oz	2oz	sprigs of fresh lavender flowers (insect free)
			or
25g	1oz	1oz	dried lavender flowers
225g	1 cup	8oz	caster sugar

Layer the sugar with the lavender flowers in a lidded jar. Leave in a warm place for 1-2 weeks, giving the jar a shake now and again to distribute the scent evenly. When the sugar has absorbed the scent of the lavender, sift it to remove the lavender flowers. Keep the jar tightly sealed and use as required.

VARIATION

Rose Petal Sugar Layer the petals of highly scented, unsprayed garden roses with caster sugar as before. Use to flavour creamy desserts, cakes, puddings and biscuits.

Vanilla Sugar

Long before Columbus reached America, the Aztec Indians were using vanilla pods as currency, medicines, perfume and in a much enjoyed drink called 'Xoco Lat', a combination of cocoa and vanilla pods. In the sixteenth century the Spanish explorer Cortes introduced vanilla to Europe where it soon became very popular.

Vanilla pods are the fruit of a climbing orchid. Their flavour develops during the curing process. The pods can be used to flavour the foods as they are, or the flavour can be extracted from them to give vanilla extract or essence. When you are buying a vanilla pod, try to find one which is covered with crystals of vanilla as this indicates freshness. Use vanilla sugar to flavour creams, custards, milk and cream puddings, cakes, sponges, whipped cream and any chocolate dishes.

Metric	US	Imperial	
1	1	1	fresh vanilla pod
450g	2¼ cups	1 lb	caster sugar

Split the vanilla pod to expose the seeds for full flavour, then place in a lidded jar with the caster sugar. Shake, then leave for 7 days. Shake again and leave for 2-3 weeks if possible, before using. Top up with more sugar when necessary.

Orange or Lemon Sugar

This is good for flavouring cakes, biscuits, puddings and creamy desserts, as it saves grating orange or lemon rinds.

Metric	US	Imperial	
3	3	3	oranges or lemons, preferably unwaxed/organic
450g	2¼ cups	1lb	caster sugar

Set the oven to its lowest temperature.

Remove the rind from the fruit with a potato peeler. You will need about 125g/4oz/4oz. Spread out on a baking sheet covered with kitchen foil. Place in the oven and leave for about 3 hours, or until dried out. Allow to cool. Layer the sugar with the dried rind in an airtight jar. Seal and label, then give the jar a shake. Keep in a cool, dark place for at least 1 week before using to allow the flavour to develop.

Cinnamon Sugar

Use to sprinkle on cakes, biscuits and puddings, or cream with butter and spread on hot fresh toast to make cinnamon toast.

Metric	US	Imperial	
450g	2¼ cups	1lb	caster sugar
50g	2oz	2oz	whole cinnamon sticks

Tip the sugar into a clean airtight jar, then press the cinnamon sticks down into the sugar. Seal and label, then give the jar a good shake. Keep in a cool, dark place for at least 1 week before using, to allow the flavour to develop.

Herb Salts

Sea salt can also be flavoured with herbs to add to savoury dishes for extra piquancy. Experiment with rosemary, tarragon, thyme, fennel, sage, basil and marjoram.

Tarragon Salt

Metric	US	Imperial	
about 50g	about 2oz	about 2oz	sprigs of fresh tarragon
125g	1 cup	4oz	sea salt

Set the oven to its lowest temperature. Strip the tarragon leaves from the stalks and discard the stalks. Coarsely chop the leaves and place in a blender. Add the sea salt and process until the leaves are finely chopped. Cover a baking sheet with kitchen foil and spread the herb mixture out on it. Place in the oven, leaving the door ajar. Leave for about 1½ hours until crisp and dry. Allow to cool, then pack into a clean airtight jar. Cover and label. Use as required.

Peppercorn and Rosemary Salt

Metric	US	Imperial	
about 15g	about ½oz	about ½oz	sprigs of fresh rosemary
7·5–12ml	½–¾ tbsp	½–¾ tbsp	mixed peppercorns
125g	1 cup	4oz	sea salt

Set the oven on its lowest temperature. Strip the rosemary leaves from the stalks and discard the stalks. Mix with the peppercorns and salt in a blender and process until the rosemary is finely chopped. Continue as for Tarragon Salt.

Flavoured Syrups

Eighteenth- and nineteenth-century recipe books often include recipes for concentrated syrups which were intended to be diluted with water when required, rather like modern squashes. Many were the descendants of the apothecary's cordials extolled for their virtues in Elizabethan books of remedies, and became favourite drinks for ladies at balls and dinners. These are an excellent way of sweetening and flavouring desserts like ice-cream, sorbets, yoghurt, fools, trifles and custards. Alternatively, a flavoured syrup can be used hot or cold as a sauce for a steamed pudding or ice-cream, as well as for drinks.

Herb and Flower Syrups

The best herbs and flowers to use for making a flavoured syrup are those with a fairly strong scent; angelica, elderflower, fennel, rose geranium and scented leaf geraniums, hyssop, lavender, lemon balm, lemon verbena, all mints, pineapple sage, rose petals, rosemary, sweet cicely and sweet violet.

Metric	US	Imperial	
225g	1 cup	8oz	caster sugar
300ml	1¼ cups	½ pint	water
4-6	4-6	4-6	sprigs of chosen herb or flower

Dissolve the sugar in the water over low heat, then bring to the boil and simmer for 3 minutes. Remove from the heat and leave to cool a little before pouring into a lidded jar or bottle. Add the herb or flower, cover the jar and allow to get completely cold. Discard the herb or flower and use the syrup as required. These syrups store in a refrigerator for two weeks, or in a freezer for 2 months. (It is easy to freeze the syrup in an ice cube tray and then wrap in individual portions.)

VARIATION

Herb and Flower-scented Wine Syrups These can be made as an alternative to plain herb or flower syrups. Instead of using all water, use half medium dry white wine and half water. Make as above.

Fruit Syrups

The best fruits for making fruit syrups are raspberries, blackberries, loganberries, strawberries, blackcurrants and elderberries. Redcurrant syrup is rather astringent, so mix the fruit with strawberries or raspberries. Dilute to make jellies and drinks, or use as sauces for ice-creams and puddings.

Metric	US	Imperial	
900g	2lb	2lb	ripe fruit
			water
			sugar

Discard any damaged fruit as well as leaves and stalks. Wash currants and elderberries, but not raspberries etc. Put the fruit in a large bowl over a saucepan of gently boiling water. Add 150ml/²⁄₃cup/¼pint water. If using currants, add 300ml/ 1¼cups/½pint. Cook for 1 hour, pressing the fruit frequently with a wooden spoon to release the juice. Strain through a jelly bag overnight.

Measure the strained juice and pour into a stainless steel or enamel pan. For every

600ml/2½ cups/1 pint juice, add 350g/1¾ cups/12oz sugar, except currants which need 450g/2 cups/1lb sugar. Stir over a low heat until the sugar has completely dissolved, then simmer for 15 minutes.

Pour the hot syrup into small, warmed, screw-top bottles, filling them to within 2·5cm/1in of the top, then screw the tops on loosely. Stand the filled bottles on a trivet or a piece of wood in a large, deep pan and wrap strips of newspaper around them for support. Fill the pan with cold water until it comes to just above the level of the syrup in the bottles. Heat the water to 77°C/170°F and maintain this temperature for at least 30 minutes to sterilise the syrup.

Remove the bottles of syrup and screw the tops on tightly. When the syrup is cold, label and store in a cool, dark, airy cupboard. It will keep well for up to 2 months.

Rose Hip Syrup

Conserves and syrups of rose hips were once made in country house still-rooms. An economical eighteenth-century recipe in the Dryden family papers at Canons Ashby makes a conserve from the pulp of 'half a peck of Hipps', then uses the left-over skin and pips to make a syrup. Rose hips make a lightly scented syrup extremely rich in vitamin C – 10ml/2tsp/2tsp daily will supply all you need. It makes an ideal addition to babies' and children's diets and a good base for a fresh fruit salad.

Metric	US	Imperial	
675g	1½lb	1½lb	rose hips
2 litres	9 cups	3½ pints	water
350g	1¾ cups	12oz	white granulated sugar

Mince the rose hips or process coarsely. Place in a pan with 1·2 litres/5 cups/2 pints of the water. Bring to the boil, then remove from the heat. Cover the pan and leave to infuse for 15 minutes. Strain through a jelly bag, then return the pulp to the saucepan, adding the remaining water. Bring to the boil again, then cover and put aside for another 15 minutes. Strain this juice through the jelly bag as before. Put into a clean pan, bring to the boil, then boil until reduced to about 600–750ml/2½–3 cups/about 1–1¼ pints. Add the sugar, stir until dissolved, then boil for a further 5 minutes. Bottle and sterilise as for Fruit Syrups (see page 70).

CHAPTER 6

Jams and Jellies

Jellies have been made from apples and soft fruit, such as raspberries, strawberries, mulberries and barberries, since Tudor and Stuart times. They were strained through a linen cloth or jelly bag, and boiled until they set with their own pectin content. They were regarded as accompaniments to meat, game and poultry rather than a spread for bread.

The word 'jam', however, did not reach the printed cookery books until 1718. Thereafter both the name and the method of preparation became common. By the late nineteenth century the first jam was manufactured outside the home, using the surplus of fruit and vegetables during the agricultural depression. Jam, spread on white bread and margarine, became part of the poor's staple diet.

The National Trust restaurants are beginning to make their own jams using local or estate fruit wherever possible, to serve with their famous cream teas. I have included some of their recipes.

Jams

Jam is a mixture of fruit and sugar cooked together until set. Pectin, a gum-like substance that occurs in varying amounts in the cell walls of fruit, is essential to setting. Acid is also necessary to help release the pectin, improve the colour and flavour, and prevent crystallisation.

Fruits rich in pectin include quinces, apples, gooseberries, damsons, redcurrants and blackcurrants; these are easily made into jam. Fruits containing a medium amount of pectin include plums, greengages, apricots, raspberries and loganberries. Those giving a poor set because of a low pectin content include rhubarb, strawberries, pears, cherries, blackberries, medlars, elderberries and rowan berries.

For a good set, jams made with fruits lacking in acid and pectin require these ingredients to be added, so they are usually mixed with another high pectin fruit. If acid is the only ingredient required, the most convenient way of adding it is in the form of lemon, redcurrant or gooseberry juice.

To Make Jam

Choosing and Preparing the Fruit

1 It should be dry, fresh and barely ripe. Over-ripe fruit does not set well.
2 Pick over the fruit discarding damaged areas or pieces of fruit and wash or wipe it.
3 Simmer gently until soft and reduced by about one-third to break down the cell walls and release the pectin. Make sure that all fruit skins are completely soft, especially thick-skinned fruits such as blackcurrants, before adding the sugar, because this will instantly toughen them.

Choosing and Using the Sugar

1 There is no keeping difference between jams made with beet sugar and sugar cane.
2 Any kind and colour of sugar (except icing sugar) will make jam, but preserving sugar makes a slightly clearer jam which needs less stirring, and produces far less scum. Brown sugars can mask the fruit flavour.
3 Commercial jam sugar, based on granulated sugar with added pectin and acid, guarantees a set for any fruit. Choose the type that guarantees a set in 4 minutes with no testing. This is useful for low pectin fruits but is expensive.
4 Warm the sugar in the oven before adding to the fruit to reduce the cooking time.
5 Take the pan off the heat before adding the sugar and stir until completely dissolved. If the mixture boils before the sugar is dissolved, it will crystallise and the jam will be crunchy and spoilt.
6 Once the sugar is dissolved completely, bring the jam to a rolling boil (one that cannot be broken down when the jam is stirred with a wooden spoon).

Testing for a Set

1 **Saucer Test:** Remove the jam from the heat and put about 2 teaspoons of jam onto a cold saucer. Allow it to cool, then push your fingertip across the centre of the jam. If the surface wrinkles well and the two halves remain separate, setting point has been reached. If not, return the pan to the heat and boil again for 5 minutes, then test again.
2 **Temperature Test:** If you have a sugar thermometer, hold it in the boiling jam, without resting it on the bottom of the pan. Bend until your eyes are level with the 104°C/220°F mark on the thermometer: this is the temperature the jam should reach when it is at setting point.
3 **Flake Test:** To double check setting point, do a quick 'flake' test. Dip the bowl of a cold wooden spoon in the jam. Take out and cool slightly, then let the jam drop from the edge of the bowl. At setting point, the jam runs together, forming flakes which break off cleanly with a shake of the spoon.
4 Most jams reach setting point between 5–20 minutes, but always start testing for a set after 5 minutes as over-boiling spoils the colour and flavour.

Potting and Covering

1 Once the setting point has been reached, pot the jam immediately, except for strawberry and raspberry jam and all marmalades. Leave these to stand for 10-15 minutes to let the fruit or rind settle, to prevent it rising to the surface in the jar.
2 Wash the jars in very hot water and dry in the oven at 140°C/275°F/gas mark 1. Leave them there until you are ready to pot the jam. The jars must be warmed before filling, or the hot jam will crack them.
3 Pour the jam into the jars using a ladle or small jug, filling them almost to the very top, leaving no space for bacteria to grow. A jam funnel makes filling easier.
4 Cover the jam immediately with waxed paper discs, placing the waxed sides down on the surface of the preserve. The surface of the jam should be completely covered by the waxed paper (buy the right size for the type of jar used). Press gently to exclude all air. Then immediately add lids or dampened cellophane covers (damp side downwards) and secure with rubber bands.

Storing

1 Stand the jars of jam aside until completely cold, then label clearly with type of jam and the date it was made.
2 Store in a cool, dark, dry and airy cupboard. Home-made jam and jelly will keep well for up to 1 year, but may deteriorate in colour and flavour if kept longer.

Apricot Jam

This is my favourite jam. My sister makes it for me as a treat – dried apricot jam is just not the same.

Metric	US	Imperial	
1·35kg	3lb	3lb	fresh apricots
			juice of 1 lemon, strained
300ml	1¼ cups	½ pint	water
1·35kg	5½ cups	3lb	sugar

Halve and stone the apricots, reserving 12 stones. Using nutcrackers, crack open the reserved stones and remove the kernels. Blanch them in boiling water for 1 minute, then drain and transfer to a bowl of cold water. Drain again, then rub off the skins with your fingers.

Simmer the apricots and kernels gently in the lemon juice and water for about 15 minutes or until the fruit is soft and the water has reduced. Add the warmed sugar and stir until it has completely dissolved, then boil rapidly for 10-15 minutes, or until setting point is reached (see page 73). Pot and cover in the usual way.

Blueberry Jam

Blueberries are distant relatives of the European bilberry and very easy to grow in your own garden.

Metric	US	Imperial	
900g	2lb	2lb	blueberries
850g	2½ cups	1¼lb	sugar
			juice of 1 lemon
			tiny pinch of salt

Put the blueberries into a china or glass bowl with half the sugar, all of the lemon juice and the salt. Stir well, then cover with a clean cloth and leave to stand overnight.

Pour the contents of the bowl into a large pan with the remaining sugar. Stir over a low heat until the sugar has completely dissolved, then increase the heat and boil rapidly for 10-12 minutes until setting point is reached (see page 73). Skim off any scum, then pot the jam in the usual way.

High Dumpsideary Jam

Although an old Gloucestershire recipe, this jam was popular all over the country in Victorian times, when it was called Mock Apricot Jam.

Metric	US	Imperial	
900g	2lb	2lb	cooking apples, peeled and cored
900g	2lb	2lb	cooking pears, peeled and cored
900g	2lb	2lb	large plums
			juice of 1 large lemon, strained
300ml	1¼ cups	½ pint	water
3	3	3	whole cloves
1	1	1	small cinnamon stick
2·75kg	6lb	6lb	sugar

Cut the apples and pears into even-sized pieces. Halve and stone the plums, reserving the stones, then place all the fruit in a large pan with the lemon juice and water. Tie the reserved plum stones, cloves and cinnamon in a piece of muslin and add to the fruit. Simmer very gently until the fruit is soft. Remove and discard the muslin bag. Add the sugar and stir until it has completely dissolved, then bring to the boil. Boil rapidly for about 15 minutes, or until setting point is reached (see page 73). Pot and cover in the usual way.

Blackberry and Apple Jam

This is one of a number of jams that the cooks at Cliveden Conservatory Restaurant make for their visitors. Use windfall or crab apples if you wish, to make a very economical jam.

Metric	US	Imperial	
900g	2lb	2lb	blackberries
150ml	2/3 cup	1/4 pint	water
450g	1lb	1lb	cooking apples
1·35kg	3lb	3lb	sugar

Place the blackberries in a large pan and add half the water, then simmer for about 15 minutes until tender. Press through a fine nylon sieve to remove all the pips, if you wish, but be sure to press through all the fruit pulp and juice for the jam. Peel, core and roughly chop the apples. Simmer gently in a separate pan with the remaining water for about 10 minutes until soft and pulpy. Place in a large pan with the blackberry pulp and sugar and stir until the sugar has dissolved. Then bring to the boil and boil rapidly for 10-15 minutes until setting point is reached (see page 73). Pot and cover in the usual way.

VARIATION

Hedgepick Jam This recipe is based on one provided by the Women's Institute during the Second World War, using fruits picked from the hedgerows. Any combination of fruits can be used but make sure that over half the quantity are fruits high in pectin i.e. crab apples, blackberries and elderberries.

Cliveden Gooseberry and Elderflower Jam

This recipe, made by the cooks at Cliveden's Conservatory Restaurant, can use any other fruit that is high in pectin. Omit the elderflowers and substitute scented geranium leaves or other herbs if you wish; for example, try blackcurrant and mint, or lemon scented geranium leaves with apple. The colour of the finished gooseberry jam will depend mainly on the variety and ripeness of the fruit used.

Metric	US	Imperial	
1·35kg	3lb	3lb	gooseberries
300ml	1¼ cups	½ pint	water
6-8	6-8	6-8	elderflower heads
1·35kg	6½ cups	3lb	sugar

Place the gooseberries in a large pan and add the water. Simmer the fruit gently for about 20 minutes, or until pulpy. Meanwhile, snip the tiny flowers off the elderflower heads, making sure they are clean and insect-free. Stir the flowers and warm sugar into the cooked fruit. Heat gently, stirring until the sugar has dissolved, then boil rapidly until setting point is reached (see page 73). Pot and cover in the usual way.

VARIATIONS

Gooseberry and Orange Jam Cook the gooseberries with the grated rind and juice of 3 oranges instead of the elderflowers.

Gooseberry and Redcurrant Jam Use 900g/2lb/2lb gooseberries and 450g/1lb/1lb redcurrants and omit the elderflowers.

Gooseberry and Strawberry Jam Use 675g/1½lb/1½lb gooseberries and 675g/ 1½lb/1½lb strawberries, cooking the fruits separately to avoid overcooking the strawberries. Omit the elderflowers.

Gooseberry and Rhubarb Jam Use 900g/2lb/2lb gooseberries and 450g/1lb/1lb chopped rhubarb. Cook the fruits separately to avoid overcooking the rhubarb, then combine them and add the sugar. Omit the elderflowers.

Rhubarb and Elderflower Jam Follow the main recipe above, using rhubarb instead of gooseberries. Rhubarb is low in pectin so use jam sugar with added pectin and follow the manufacturer's instructions for boiling.

Kea Plum Jam

Kea plums grow on the banks of the River Fal near Trelissick Garden in Cornwall. They are a damson variety; small, dark and excellent for jam-making. The harvest used to continue throughout August and September 'with all hands available for shaking, picking, sorting and counting'. So many trees overhung the creeks that it used to be possible to shake the plums directly into boats. Ferns were used to line the baskets to protect and preserve the fruit (a trick also used when picking blackberries).

The restaurant at Trelissick buys much of the present crop for making jam to serve with their afternoon teas. Use a good-flavoured plum, preferably home grown, or damsons.

Metric	US	Imperial	
1·35kg	3lb	3lb	plums, washed
150ml	²/₃ cup	¼ pint	water
1·35kg	6½ cups	3lb	sugar

If using large plums, halve and stone them, discarding the stones. Place the plums in a pan and add the water. Simmer very gently until the fruit is very soft and the liquid has reduced by about two-thirds. Stir in the sugar and heat gently, stirring until all the sugar has dissolved, then boil rapidly for about 15 minutes or until setting point is reached (see page 73). Remove the pan from the heat and use a draining spoon to remove the stones. Pot and cover in the usual way.

Hidcote Raspberry Jam

This jam is made in the kitchen of Hidcote Garden Restaurant using locally picked raspberries. Loganberries or tayberries can be used instead.

Metric	US	Imperial	
1·35kg	3lb	3lb	raspberries, preferably under-ripe
1·35kg	6½ cups	3lb	sugar

Place the raspberries in a large pan and heat very gently until the juices start to run. Gently shake the pan from side to side trying not to break the fruit up too much. Leave to simmer very slowly for about 20 minutes, or until the fruit is cooked. Add the warmed sugar and stir gently over a low heat until the sugar has completely dissolved. Bring to the boil and boil rapidly until setting point is reached (see page 73). Pot and cover in the usual way.

VARIATION

Hidcote Raspberry and Mead Conserve Add 175ml/³/₄ cup/6 fl oz of mead (this is the equivalent of ¼ bottle) to 2·75kg/6lb/6lb raspberries in the first stage of cooking. Use 2·75kg/13 cups/6lb sugar.

Uncooked Raspberry Conserve

If you have some perfect, freshly-picked raspberries, use this uncooked method to make a special soft-set conserve, which should be used within 1 month. Keep the jars in the refrigerator once opened.

Metric	US	Imperial	
1kg	2¼lb	2¼lb	raspberries
1·25kg	6 cups	2¾lb	caster sugar

Preheat the oven to 180°C/350°F/gas mark 4.

Place the raspberries and sugar in separate ovenproof bowls. Put both bowls in the oven for about 20 minutes, until the contents of each is hot. Quickly and thoroughly stir the fruit and sugar together until all the sugar has dissolved, lightly crushing the fruit as you do so. Pot and cover in the usual way.

VARIATIONS

Uncooked Strawberry Conserve Use strawberries instead of raspberries.

Uncooked Raspberry and Redcurrant Conserve Replace 450g/1lb/1lb raspberries with an equal weight of redcurrants.

Rhubarb and Ginger Jam

This is an old-fashioned preserve which is made in the kitchen of Cliveden's Conservatory Restaurant.

Metric	US	Imperial	
1·8kg	4lb	4lb	rhubarb, trimmed and cut into 2·5cm/1in pieces
1·8kg	9 cups	4lb	sugar
			grated rind and juice of 2 lemons, preferably unwaxed/organic
50g	2oz	2oz	bruised root ginger
50g	2oz	2oz	preserved stem ginger, chopped

Put the rhubarb in a large bowl, layering it with the sugar, the lemon rind and juice. Cover with a cloth and leave to stand overnight.

Turn the soaked fruit and all its juice into a preserving pan and add the bruised root ginger tied in a piece of muslin. Simmer gently until the fruit is soft and pulpy, stirring frequently to dissolve the sugar completely. Boil rapidly to setting point (see page 73). Remove the muslin bag of ginger. Stir in the chopped stem ginger, then pot and cover in the usual way.

Strawberry Jam

This is the jam everyone loves, young and old, and it is the traditional one served with the famous National Trust cream tea. Strawberries are low in both pectin and acid, so additional pectin is usually supplied; the easiest way is to use ready-prepared jam sugar with added pectin. Raspberries, loganberries or tayberries can be treated in the same way.

Use as many small strawberries as you can find. They should be freshly picked and top quality to make this superior preserve. Even though it takes several days to prepare, it is extremely easy to make.

Metric	US	Imperial	
1·35kg	3 lb	3 lb	small strawberries
1·35kg	6½ cups	3 lb	sugar
			juice of 1 lemon

Hull the strawberries and layer with two-thirds of the sugar in a wide, shallow china or glass bowl. Sprinkle over the remaining sugar. Cover with clingfilm and leave at room temperature (as long as your room is not too warm) for 24 hours.

Transfer the strawberries and their syrup to a preserving pan, scraping any undissolved sugar into the pan. Add the lemon juice. Bring slowly to the boil, allow the mixture to bubble over a low heat for 5 minutes, then remove from the heat. Cover and leave, again at room temperature, for 48 hours.

Return the pan to the heat and bring back to the boil. Boil for about 10–15 minutes until setting point is reached (see page 73). Remove the pan from the heat and skim off any scum. Cool for 10 minutes, before potting and covering in the usual way.

Crystallised flowers and herbs: Rose Petals, Violets, Primroses and Rosemary. (*NTPL/Andreas von Einsiedel*)

Jellies

Only the juice of fruit is used for jelly-making, so the yield is much lower than that of jam. The best fruits are those with a strong natural flavour, such as redcurrants, blackcurrants, blackberries, elderberries and damsons. A good pectin content is essential, so fruit with a good flavour but modest pectin content, are usually combined with ingredients that are rich in pectin. Cooking apples (windfalls can be used) and crab apples are both excellent for their pectin content, especially when a second ingredient – another fruit or herb – is added to give extra flavour and colour. Quinces combine high pectin content with good flavour, and these make successful jellies.

Piquant herb jellies, sharpened with vinegar, are versatile accompaniments to fish, roast meats, poultry and game, cold cuts and raised pork or game pies. They can be based on apple juice, made from cooking apples, windfalls or crab apples, or orange and/or lemon juice. The most successful herb jellies are sage, mint, scented geranium, lemon balm, marjoram, rosemary, oregano, thyme and basil, but do experiment. The herbs can be chopped or added in sprigs.

A good jelly should be clear, sparkling and full of flavour. It should retain its shape when cut, but should not be too stiff to spread like jam. As well as using jelly in all the sweet roles familiar to jam, they can also be used in marinades or for basting grilled and roast meat during the final stages of cooking. Fragrant home-made jellies make very attractive presents.

To Make Jelly

Choosing and Preparing the Fruit

1 The fruit should never be over-ripe because a good set is achieved when acid, sugar and pectin are present in the correct proportions. There is more acid and pectin in under-ripe fruit.
2 Discard any bruised or damaged fruit. It is not necessary to remove peel, cores and stalks, as they will be extracted when the pulp is strained. Wash the fruit.
3 Cook in water, with any spices, according to the recipe to release the acid and pectin, stirring and mashing frequently with a potato masher, until the fruit is very soft and pulpy.

Crystallised fruit: Tangerines, Orange Slices and Plums.
(*NTPL/Andreas von Einsiedel*)

Straining the Fruit

1 Scald a jelly bag in boiling water and suspend it over a large, perfectly clean bowl. (Use a jelly bag stand for this or an upturned stool.)
2 Spoon the fruit pulp into the bag and leave to drain for at least 4 hours, preferably overnight. Let the juice drip naturally (if you squeeze the bag or push the juice through, the jelly will be cloudy). The juice is not clear when strained from the fruit, but it clears on boiling with sugar.

Completing the Jelly

1 Measure the strained juice and weigh out the sugar, generally 450g/2¼ cups/1lb sugar for each 600ml/2½ cups/1 pint juice. Slightly less or more sugar can be added for fruit with lower or higher than average pectin contents.
2 Warm the sugar as for jam (see page 73).
3 Put the juice into a clean, heavy-based pan and heat gently with the sugar, stirring until the sugar has completely dissolved. Boil rapidly until setting point is reached (see page 73).
4 Remove the pan from the heat, then skim off any scum from the surface with a draining spoon. Any remaining scum can be removed by drawing a piece of kitchen paper across the top. Adding a knob of butter just before skimming helps to disperse the scum.
5 Pour the jelly very gently into warmed sterilised jars. Don't pour too quickly or this will create bubbles in the jelly. Cover and label as for jam (see page 74). Take care not to move the jars while the jelly is setting, or it will split.

Basic Apple Juice

Metric	US	Imperial	
3·6kg	8lb	8lb	apples, roughly chopped
300ml	1¼ cups	½ pint	white wine vinegar or cider vinegar
			juice of 6 large lemons
1·2 litres	5 cups	2 pints	water

Place the prepared apples in a preserving pan. Add the vinegar, lemon juice and water. Simmer for about 45 minutes, or until the apples are soft and pulpy. Strain through a jelly bag overnight.

Mint or Sage Jelly

Metric	US	Imperial	
15g	1/2 oz	1/2 oz	fresh mint or sage leaves
900ml	4 cups	1 1/2 pints	apple juice (see page 82)
675g	2 3/4 cups	1 1/2 lb	sugar
			natural green food colouring (optional)

Blanch the mint or sage leaves in boiling water for 2–3 seconds, then drain and rinse under cold water. Drain again and pat dry with kitchen paper then finely chop the herbs (there should be about 15ml/1tbsp/1tbsp). Pour the apple juice into a pan, add the warmed sugar and stir over gentle heat until it has dissolved completely. Boil rapidly for 5–10 minutes or until setting point is reached (see page 73). Remove from the heat, skim, then stir in the chopped mint or sage and a few drops of green colouring if using. Pot, cover and store.

VARIATION

Herb Garden Jelly Use a mixture of fresh herbs to make this savoury jelly that goes well with a variety of meats, poultry or fish. Follow the above recipe, but use a combination of fresh parsley, mint, thyme and tarragon. To balance the flavour of the herbs, use more parsley and mint than the stronger thyme and tarragon.

Rosemary, Thyme, Basil or Marjoram Jelly

Metric	US	Imperial	
8–10	8–10	8–10	small fresh sprigs of your chosen herb
2	2	2	large fresh sprigs of your chosen herb
900ml	4 cups	1 1/2 pints	apple juice (see page 82)
675g	2 3/4 cups	1 1/2 lb	sugar

Blanch the small sprigs of herbs in boiling water for 2–3 seconds, rinse under cold water, pat dry with kitchen paper and reserve. Wash the large sprigs of herbs and dry them. Make the jelly as for Mint or Sage Jelly, adding the large herb sprigs while dissolving the sugar. Remove the herbs and boil until setting point is reached (see page 73). Put the reserved small herb sprigs into sterilised jars, then pour in the jelly. Cover and store as for jam (see page 74).

Apple Geranium Jelly

Use scented geranium leaves to make this unusual jelly.

Metric	US	Imperial	
6	6	6	scented geranium leaves
900ml	4 cups	1½ pints	apple juice (see page 82)
675g	2¾ cups	1½ lb	white sugar

Wash and dry the geranium leaves, then tie them in a piece of muslin. Pour the apple juice into a pan and add the warmed sugar and the muslin bag. Stir over a very gentle heat until the sugar has completely dissolved. Boil rapidly for 5-10 minutes, or until setting point is reached (see page 73). Remove from the heat and discard the muslin bag. Skim, then pot and cover.

Orange and Thyme Jelly

This herb jelly is best with a mixture of orange and lemon juice rather than apple.

Metric	US	Imperial	
900g	2 lb	2 lb	oranges, preferably unwaxed / organic
900g	2 lb	2 lb	lemons, preferably unwaxed / organic
2 litres	8 cups	3½ pints	water
			sugar
60ml	¼ cup	4 tbsp	fresh thyme leaves

Wash and slices the oranges and lemons. Cut the slices into halves or quarters and place in a large pan. Pour on the water, then bring to the boil. Simmer gently for about 1 hour, or until the fruit is soft. Strain through a jelly bag overnight.

   Measure the juice and pour into a large pan. Add warmed sugar, allowing 450g/ 2¼ cups / 1 lb sugar for every 600ml / 2½ cups / 1 pint juice. Heat gently, stirring until the sugar has completely dissolved. Bring to the boil, then boil rapidly until setting point is reached (see page 73). Remove any scum immediately, then stir in the thyme leaves. Cool slightly until a thin skin forms on the surface, then stir gently to distribute the thyme leaves. Pot and cover.

My Sister's Bramble Jelly

This is my very favourite jelly. Cheap and simple to make, it has such a wonderfully evocative flavour. Spread on thick slices of freshly baked bread and scones, or serve with poultry or game birds.

Metric	US	Imperial	
900g	2lb	2lb	blackberries
225ml	¾ cup	7½ fl oz	water
			juice of 1 lemon
400g	2 cups	14oz	sugar

Wash the blackberries, then place them in a pan with the water and lemon juice. Bring to the boil then simmer for about 20 minutes, until very soft, crushing with a potato masher. Strain the fruit through a jelly bag overnight.

Pour the juice into a clean pan. Add the warmed sugar and stir over a gentle heat until the sugar has completely dissolved. Increase the heat and bring to the boil. Boil rapidly for about 7 minutes or until setting point is reached (see page 73). Skim, then pot and cover.

VARIATION

Spiced Bramble Jelly Tie 15ml/1tbsp/1tbsp of whole cloves and 1 cinnamon stick lightly crushed in a square of muslin and add to the initial cooking of the blackberries.

Damson Jelly

Beatrix Potter made damson jelly every September using damsons gathered from the orchards at Hill Top, her farmhouse in Cumbria. The fruit is so rich in pectin and acid that it invariably makes a very good jelly. Spread on bread, scones, muffins and crumpets, or use as an accompaniment to poultry, ham, lamb or mutton. Beatrix served hers with the local Herdwick lamb or mutton, which is still being raised on the farms she left to the National Trust.

Metric	US	Imperial	
1·8kg	4lb	4lb	damsons
900ml	4 cups	1½ pints	water
			sugar

Place the damsons in a large pan with the water for about 40 minutes until very soft and pulpy, crushing with a potato masher from time to time. Strain through a jelly bag overnight. Measure the strained liquid and pour it into a clean pan with 450g/2¼ cups/1lb warmed sugar for each 600ml/2½ cups/1 pint. Heat gently, stirring, until the sugar has dissolved, then boil rapidly until setting point is reached (see page 73). Start testing after 3–4 minutes. Skim, then pot and cover.

VARIATIONS

Spiced Damson Jelly Tie 4 whole cloves and cinnamon stick in a piece of muslin and put into the pan with the damsons and water. Continue as above.

Blackcurrant Jelly Substitute blackcurrants for the damsons and use 1·2 litres/ 5 cups/2 pints water. Blackcurrant is delicious with duck or goose.

Gooseberry Jelly Use gooseberries instead of damsons. Excellent with smoked fish.

Gooseberry and Elderflower Jelly Make as above, but include a muslin bag of 8 elderflower heads with the gooseberries during the initial cooking.

Hedgerow Jelly

At Erddig Ellen Jefferies is famous for her spiced jellies made from fruits gathered from the hedgerow or grown in her orchard and garden. She sets up her stall every October on Apple Day, which the restaurant also celebrates by serving local apple dishes. Try different combinations of fruits as Ellen does, remembering that you will need apple, lemon juice or commercial pectin to ensure a good set when using fruit low in pectin or acid, such as elderberries, blackberries and sloes.

Metric	US	Imperial	
900g	2lb	2lb	blackberries
900g	2lb	2lb	elderberries
900g	2lb	2lb	crab apples, washed and cut in half
15ml	1tbsp	1tbsp	cloves
1	1	1	cinnamon stick, lightly crushed
2·1 litres	9 cups	3½ pints	water
			white sugar

Pick over all the fruit and place in a large pan with the spices and water. Bring to the boil, then simmer gently for about 45 minutes until the fruits are very soft, stirring occasionally with a wooden spoon and crushing with a potato masher. Strain through a jelly bag overnight.

Measure the juice and pour it into a pan with 450g/2¼ cups/1lb warmed sugar to each 600ml/2½ cups/1 pint. Heat gently, stirring until the sugar has dissolved, then boil rapidly for 10–15 minutes until setting point is reached (see page 73). Skim, then pot and cover.

Old-fashioned Quince Jelly

This very fine, deep-pink jelly has been made since Elizabethan days. It is extremely versatile; try serving it with a full-flavoured cheese and crusty home-made bread, or offer it with roast lamb, mutton, game or ham. It is also excellent topped with cream as a filling for sponge cakes or spread on scones and muffins, in the same way as jams. It makes a sparkling glaze for fruit flans and cheesecakes. Precious quinces can be eked out by adding a portion of windfall apples or crab apples.

Metric	US	Imperial	
1·35kg	3lb	3lb	quinces
1·7 litres	7½ cups	3 pints	water
			thinly pared rind and juice of 1 large lemon
			preferably unwaxed/organic
			sugar

Wash the quinces and rub off the soft down on their skins. Cut up roughly and place in a large pan with the water, lemon rind and lemon juice. Simmer for 1½–2 hours or until the fruit is very soft and pulpy. Strain through a jelly bag overnight.

Measure the juice and pour into a clean pan. Add warmed sugar, allowing 450g/ 2¼ cups/1lb to each 600ml/2½ cups/1 pint juice, then heat gently, stirring until the sugar is dissolved. Boil rapidly until setting point is reached (see page 73). Begin testing after 3–4 minutes. Skim, then pot and cover.

VARIATIONS

Japonica Jelly Substitute japonicas (chaenomales), which are a closely related species to the quince.

Medlar Jelly Substitute medlars for the quinces, but use them before they get to the softened, bloated stage. The jelly is excellent with poultry and game.

Superlative Redcurrant Jelly

This recipe is based on one first published in 1840 by Eliza Acton in her famous *Modern Cookery for Private Families*. It is very easy and results in a jewel-bright and fruity jelly. In the eighteenth and early nineteenth centuries, redcurrant jelly was the recommended condiment to serve with hare and venison, but now we also enjoy it with lamb. Use also as a glaze for flans and cheesecakes and in sauces such as Cumberland.

Metric	US	Imperial	
900g	2lb	2lb	redcurrants
900g	4¼ cups	2lb	sugar

Wash the fruit, but don't bother to strip from the stalks. Run a film of water over the base of a large pan, then add the redcurrants and warmed sugar. Heat very slowly, stirring until the sugar has completely dissolved, then boil rapidly for a few minutes, until setting point is reached (see page 73). Tip into a nylon sieve lined with a double layer of muslin over a bowl, then pour the jelly into sterilised jars. Cover and label.

Spiced Redcurrant Jelly Add 3 whole cloves and 1 stick of cinnamon lightly crushed to the redcurrants.

Redcurrant and Port Jelly Boil the strained jelly with 125ml/½ cup/4 fl oz port before potting.

Redcurrant and Whitecurrant Jelly Use a combination of redcurrants and whitecurrants to make a milder, less sharp jelly. This is good with roast lamb and for adding to sauces.

Redcurrant and Raspberry Jelly Use 450g/1lb/1lb redcurrants and 450g/1lb/1lb raspberries.

Rowan and Crab Apple Jelly

Rowanberries, the fruit of the mountain ash, which is common throughout Britain, are best picked in October. They make the most delicious, tangy, orange-red jelly, which is the traditional and best accompaniment for venison, grouse and hare. I also like to serve it with mutton, lamb or goose. Adding apples improves the set – use cooking apples instead of crab apples if you wish.

Metric	US	Imperial	
900g	2lb	2lb	rowanberries
900g	2lb	2lb	crab apples
			white sugar

Remove the rowanberries from their stalks and wash well. Cut up the apples roughly and place both fruits in a pan with just enough water to cover them. Simmer gently for about 45 minutes, or until the fruit is very soft, crushing with a potato masher, then strain through a jelly bag overnight.

Measure the juice and pour into a clean pan with the warmed sugar, allowing 450g/2¼ cups/1lb to each 600ml/2½ cups/1 pint. Heat gently until the sugar has dissolved, then boil rapidly for about 10 minutes, or until setting point is reached (see page 73). Pot and cover.

VARIATIONS

Sloe and Crab Apple Jelly Use sloes instead of rowanberries to make a tangy jelly, especially good with mutton, rabbit or hare.

Elderberry, Bilberry or Cranberry and Crab Apple Jelly Substitute elderberries, bilberries or cranberries for the rowanberries. This is particularly good with turkey, guinea fowl or pheasant.

Damson and Crab Apple Jelly Use damsons instead of rowanberries.

CHAPTER 7

Fruit Butters, Cheeses, Pastes and Curds

These preserves are all basically the same mixture, but are cooked to a different consistency and with varying proportions of sugar. A large quantity of fruit yields only a relatively small amount of finished preserve, but they have a concentrated flavour.

To Make Fruit Butters, Cheese and Pastes

1 A very wide range of fruit can be used. Simmer it until soft and pulpy.
2 Rub the cooked fruit through a fine nylon sieve to make a pulp, leaving only a debris of pips, stones and skins.
3 Weigh the pulp and put in a pan with the appropriate amount of sugar.
4 Boil rapidly until the required consistency is reached and then pot as for jam or pack in the appropriate way and store in a dry, dark place.

Firm cheeses are packed into wide-topped jars or containers so that they can be unmoulded and sliced for serving. This chapter also includes fruit curds. They are similar to pastes only in that they are smooth, with a spreading texture, but they are made from fresh eggs and butter, and do not keep for long.

Fruit Butters

These have a soft butter-like consistency and can be used in the same way as jam. They are delicious spread on bread and butter, or served with scones and cream. They also make excellent fillings for sponges and tarts.

Fruit Butters are made by the addition of 225g–350g / 1–1³/₄ cups / 8oz–12oz sugar to every 450g / 1lb / 1lb fruit pulp. They should be put into small, warm, sterilised jars or pots and covered as for jam (see page 74). Fruit butters will keep for only 3–6 months without spoiling as they have a lower sugar content than fruit cheese, so they should be made in small batches.

Spiced Apple Butter

This is one of the oldest recipes for a fruit butter. It is very like the nineteenth-century apple 'marmalade' which was said to be 'very nice, and extremely wholesome as supper for the juveniles, and for the aged, eaten with cream or milk'. Spread it on crusty bread and butter or hot buttered muffins.

Metric	US	Imperial	
2·75kg	6lb	6lb	apples (windfalls or crab apples can be used)
1·2 litres	5 cups	2 pints	water
1·2 litres	5 cups	2 pints	sweet cider
2·5ml	½tsp	½tsp	ground allspice
5ml	1 tsp	1 tsp	ground cloves
10ml	2 tsp	2 tsp	ground cinnamon
			sugar

Wash the apples thoroughly and remove their stalks with any bruised parts. Chop the fruit roughly, place in the pan with the water and cider, then bring to the boil. Cover the pan and simmer until the apples are soft and pulpy, stirring frequently. Rub the apple pulp through a fine nylon sieve, then weigh it and return to the pan. Allow 350g/1¾ cups/12oz sugar for each 450g/1lb/1lb apple pulp and add to the pan with the spices. Bring gently to the boil, stirring frequently until the sugar has dissolved. Continue boiling, stirring occasionally, until the mixture thickens and there is no extra liquid left in the pan. Put the butter into hot clean jars and cover immediately.

VARIATIONS

Apple Ginger Butter Instead of the allspice cloves and cinnamon, use 10ml/2tsp/ 2tsp ground ginger.

Cidered Apple Butter Use all cider instead of a mixture of cider and water.

Bramble and Apple Butter

This is heavenly spread thickly on scones and Cornish or Devonshire splits, with clotted cream. It is also good with cold roast or as an accompaniment for cream cheese at the end of a meal.

Metric	US	Imperial	
900g	2lb	2lb	blackberries
900g	2lb	2lb	cooking apples
			grated rind and juice of 2 lemons
			sugar

Wash the fruit and chop the apples roughly, including peel and cores. Place in a pan with lemon rind and juice, then simmer gently for about 15 minutes, or until very soft. Rub through a fine nylon sieve and weigh the pulp. Replace the pulp in the pan and add sugar, allowing 350g/1¾cups/12oz sugar to each 450g/1lb/1lb blackberry pulp. Continue as for Spiced Apple Butter (see page 90).

Plum Butter

Any variety of plum makes good butter, particularly dark-skinned fruit. A similar butter can be made using damsons. As well as being superb in the usual sweet-preserve roles, they can be used as a standby for making plum sauce in Chinese cookery.

Metric	US	Imperial	
1·8kg	4lb	4lb	ripe plums
			sugar

Wash the plums and slit the skins. Put in a pan with a little water and simmer gently for about 20 minutes, or until very soft. Press through a nylon sieve until only the skins and stones are left. Weigh the pulp and replace in the pan with the appropriate amount of sugar, allowing 350g/1¾cups/12oz sugar to each 450g/1lb/1lb plum pulp. Continue as for Spiced Apple Butter (see page 90).

Rhubarb and Orange Butter

Metric	US	Imperial	
1·8kg	4lb	4lb	rhubarb, trimmed and roughly chopped
4	4	4	oranges, preferably unwaxed/organic
			sugar

Peel the oranges thinly with a sharp knife or potato peeler, taking only the zest and none of the pith. Cut the oranges in half and squeeze out the juice. Place the rhubarb in a pan with the peel and juice of the oranges. Add enough water just to cover the fruit. Bring to the boil, cover the pan and simmer until the rhubarb is very tender. Rub the pulp through a fine sieve. Weigh and allow 225g/1cup/8oz sugar for each 450g/1lb/1lb pulp. Continue as for Spiced Apple Butter (see page 90).

Blackberry, Apple, Orange and Juniper Butter

Spread on toasted muffins or crumpets, or eat with cold roast pork or baked ham.

Metric	US	Imperial	
1 kg	2¼ lb	2¼ lb	cooking apples
600 g	1 lb 5 oz	1 lb 5 oz	blackberries
4	4	4	oranges, preferably unwaxed/organic
4	4	4	lemons, preferably unwaxed/organic
300 ml	1¼ cups	½ pint	cranberry juice
5 ml	1 tsp	1 tsp	juniper berries, crushed
			sugar

Roughly chop the apples (peel, cores and all) and place in a large pan with the blackberries. Remove the peel from the oranges and discard; chop the flesh. Squeeze the juice from the lemons. Add the orange flesh, lemon juice and lemon skins to the pan. Pour over the cranberry juice and add the juniper berries. Bring gently to the boil and simmer until the fruit is soft and pulpy. Remove the lemon skins and leave to cool. Push the pulp through a nylon sieve and weigh. Place in a pan with the sugar, allowing 350g/1¾ cups/12oz sugar to every 450g/1lb/1lb pulp. Continue as for Spiced Apple Butter (see page 90).

Fruit Cheeses

These are much thicker than butters. They should be cooked until the mixture is so thick that if a spoon is drawn across the base of the pan, it will leave a definite path. Use small straight-sided jars or moulds so that the cheese can be turned out whole. Before potting, brush the inside of the warmed jars or moulds with a little tasteless oil (sweet almond or grapeseed, for example) or glycerine to make unmoulding easier. Pour in the hot cheese and cover as for jam.

A fruit cheese should be kept for at least 6 months before opening but, once it has been turned out, it should be used up as quickly as possible. (In a pot, they will keep for at least 2 years, improving all the time.) Fruit cheeses are usually sliced or cut into wedges and eaten with meat, poultry (particularly smoked), game, raised pies or with dairy cheeses.

Crab Apple Cheese

Crab apple or apple cheese was a feature of Victorian dinner tables, especially at Christmas time, when it was eaten as a dessert decorated with whole hazelnuts and whipped cream. The best is made with one type of apple only.

Metric	US	Imperial	
1·35kg	3lb	3lb	crab apples or windfall apples
			sugar

Wash and chop the apples across the core to expose the pips – this is important for the flavour of the cheese. Put into a large pan and cover with water. Cook until really soft, then strain through a jelly bag overnight.

Reserve the juice to make jelly. Push the remaining pulp through a fine sieve and place in a clean pan with the sugar, allowing 450g/2¼ cups/1lb to each 450g/1lb/1lb apple pulp. Bring slowly to the boil, stirring frequently, until the sugar is dissolved. Continue boiling, stirring regularly, until the mixture is so thick that when you draw a wooden spoon across the bottom of the pan, it leaves a clean line. Pot and store (see page 89).

Eat the cheese as a dessert with thick cream poured over it. As an accompaniment to cold roast pork, ham, goose, duck or game, turn out whole and slice at the table.

VARIATIONS

Spiced Crab Apple Cheese Add 2·5ml/½tsp/½tsp ground cloves and 2·5ml/½tsp/½tsp ground cinnamon to the apple pulp.

Apple and Blackberry Cheese Substitute 450g/1lb/1lb blackberries for 450g/1lb/1lb apples. Serve with cold pheasant or other game.

Apple and Plum Cheese Substitute 450g/1lb/1lb plums for 450g/1lb/1lb apples. Serve with hot or cold roast lamb or duck.

Apple, Plum and Mint Cheese Make as for Apple and Plum Cheese, but just before the cheese is ready, stir in 60ml/¼cup/4tbsp chopped mint leaves. Cook for a further 5 minutes and pot as before. Serve with hot or cold roast lamb or duck.

Apple and Mint Cheese Make as for Apple Cheese, but add 60ml/¼cup/4tbsp chopped fresh mint just before it is ready. Cook for 5 minutes and pot as before. Serve with hot or cold roast lamb.

Apple and Sage Cheese Make as for Apple Cheese, but add 60ml/¼cup/4tbsp chopped fresh sage just before it is ready. Serve with hot or cold roast pork or duck.

Damson Cheese

This cheese is one of the oldest traditional country dishes, always found piled up on the shelves of a country store cupboard. The cheese, if properly made, is a dark purple, almost black, and should keep for years. It is at its best when it has shrunk a little from the sides of the jars and the top has begun to crust with sugar.

In the old days, damson cheeses were often poured into deep dinner plates or large shallow pots and stored for several days in a dry, dark cupboard. They were then turned out, stacked one on top of each other with bay leaves in between and covered with muslin or cheesecloth. They were kept like this until crusted with sugar and then brought out for dessert at a special dinner party, often at Christmas, when they were studded with almonds and served with a little port wine poured over.

Metric	US	Imperial	
1·35kg	3lb	3lb	damsons
150ml	2/3 cup	1/4 pint	water
			sugar

Wash the fruit, then simmer gently with the water until soft and pulpy. Rub through a fine sieve, weigh the pulp, then return to pan. Crack a few stones and remove the kernels. Chop these and add to the damson pulp. (The kernels give an almond flavour to the finished cheese.) Continue as for Crab Apple Cheese (see page 93). Serve either as a dessert, or thickly sliced as an accompaniment to cold roast lamb, turkey or pheasant.

VARIATIONS

Damson and Mint Cheese Add 45ml/3tbsp/3tbsp chopped fresh mint just before the cheese is cooked. Cook for a further 5 minutes and pot as before. Serve with hot or cold roast pork or lamb or with game.

Plum or Sloe Cheese Substitute plums or sloes for the damsons.

Quince Cheese

This cheese has a lovely honey flavour reminding you of warm summer days. It is very good with crusty bread, cold poultry or ham, or as an accompaniment to cheese.

Metric	US	Imperial	
1·35kg	3lb	3lb	quinces, chopped
			sugar

Make as for Crab Apple Cheese (see page 93).

Spiced Cranberry and Apple Cheese

The cranberry was an English fruit taken to America by the first settlers and absorbed into their cookery. It used to flourish in the East Anglian Fens before these were drained, but now is very rare, growing only in the north of England, Scotland and Wales. Cranberry cheese is good with cold poultry and game, especially at Christmas. The cheese looks good turned out and left whole, then decorated with orange slices.

Metric	US	Imperial	
450g	1lb	1lb	cranberries
450g	1lb	1lb	cooking apples
			grated rind and juice of 2 oranges, preferably unwaxed/organic
1	1	1	blade of mace
2·5ml	½tsp	½tsp	whole cloves
½	½	½	cinnamon stick
300ml	1¼ cups	½ pint	water
			sugar

Wash the cranberries and wash and chop the apples, including their peel and cores. Place in a pan with the orange rind and juice and the spices. Pour over the water and cover the pan. Bring to the boil, then simmer for about 30 minutes, or until the fruit is soft and pulpy. Rub through a nylon sieve and weigh the pulp. Place in a clean pan and add 450g/2¼ cups/1lb sugar for every 450g/1lb/1lb fruit pulp. Continue to cook and pot as for Crab Apple Cheese (see page 93).

Green Gooseberry Cheese

Apparently this cheese was popular in Jane Austen's household. It is very good served with smoked fish, especially mackerel, or with cold meats, particularly lamb, goose or smoked duck. It also makes a refreshing and summery dessert, coated with pouring cream.

Metric	US	Imperial	
1·35kg	3lb	3lb	green gooseberries
about 300ml	about 1¼ cups	about ½ pint	water
			sugar

Wash the fruit, then cook gently in the water until soft and pulpy. Continue as for Crab Apple Cheese (see page 93).

Fruit Pastes

Apple, plum, apricot and quince pastes or 'comfits' (rather like today's fruit pastilles) were popular sweetmeats in Tudor and Stuart times. They were cut into shapes, then rolled in sugar and kept in special cupboards for use during the winter when fresh fruit was scarce.

The mixture for fruit pastes is the same as for a fruit cheese, but the cooking is continued, stirring all the time, until almost dry. The cold mixture will be about the consistency of soft marzipan. Shape the paste into balls, or oblongs, and wrap in waxed paper to be served as confectionery, or place in paper sweet cases in a pretty box as an unusual gift.

Quince Comfits

Quinces are often to be seen growing in National Trust gardens or orchards. Attingham Park, near Shrewsbury, produces fine quinces in a good year and Oxburgh Hall has a quince orchard. The restaurant celebrates the quince harvest with an evening of quince dishes, rounded off with these comfits.

Metric	US	Imperial	
450g	1lb	1lb	very ripe quinces
150ml	²/₃ cup	¼ pint	medium sweet wine
			sugar
			a little ground cinnamon
			a little ground ginger
			a little black pepper
			caster sugar to finish

Cut up the quinces roughly, including the skin and cores. Simmer with the wine until very tender, then rub through a nylon sieve. Weigh the pulp and return to a clean pan with an equal amount of sugar. Season to taste with the spices, then bring slowly to the boil, stirring frequently to dissolve the sugar. Cook gently for about 1¹/₂ hours, until the mixture is very thick indeed and leaving the side of the pan. Stir frequently to prevent it from burning. Remove from the heat, then leave to cool completely.

Roll small pieces in caster sugar. Store in a wooden or cardboard box lined with waxed paper with extra caster sugar to prevent the sweets from sticking together.

Apricot Paste

This recipe is taken from a commonplace book written in 1699 by Elizabeth Birkett of Townend, near Windermere in Cumbria. She was the wife of a wealthy yeoman farmer – one of the Browne family who lived in the house from 1626 until 1944. The original recipe mixes a pound of apricot pulp with half a pound of apple pulp to bulk out an expensive fruit, but I think the flavour is better using just apricots.

Metric	US	Imperial	
225g	8oz	8oz	dried apricots (ready-to-eat type)
450ml	1¹/₂ cups	³/₄ pint	warm water
			sugar
15ml	1 tbsp	1 tbsp	lemon juice
			caster sugar to finish

Soak the apricots in the water for at least 4 hours. Place in a saucepan and cook very gently over a low heat for 20–30 minutes, or until very soft. Purée the apricots with the water in a blender or food processor, or sieve them. Weigh the pulp and return it to a clean pan with an equal amount of sugar and the lemon juice. Stir over a low heat until the sugar has completely dissolved, then increase the heat and cook the mixture, stirring occasionally, until thick enough to almost leave the sides of the pan.

Turn into a lightly buttered non-stick baking tin (20 × 15cm / 8 × 6in) and place in a very low oven for 1-2 hours until the paste is dry enough to be cut into squares or alternatively, leave the paste in a warm room for 2-4 days. Roll in caster sugar and arrange in sweet cases in a pretty box.

Fruit Curds

These contain butter and eggs, so have a limited shelf life and should be kept in the refrigerator for up to 6 weeks. Even when stored in the refrigerator, it is a good idea to inspect them occasionally for signs of mould.

Fruit curds were originally made in stone pots standing in a pan of hot water, then stored in these pots on the still-room or store cupboard shelf. The nearest modern equivalent to this method is to make the curd in a slow cooker, which is really easy, (see Trelissick Lemon Curd on page 100). Alternatively, fruit curds can be made very successfully in a basin over a pan of hot water, or in a double saucepan. You do have to keep an eye on them in case they curdle. If this has just began to happen, remove quickly from the heat and stand in a bowl of cold water. Whisk hard until the curdling has disappeared. Continue to heat until thick enough to coat the back of a wooden spoon and hold a light ribbon trail. Don't overcook the curd as it will thicken on cooking. A good curd should have a smooth consistency with a fresh flavour.

Mayfield Apple Curd

This makes a delectable filling for tarts and sponge cakes, especially with whipped cream. It is also good spread thickly on fresh bread and scones, which is how we first enjoyed this particular curd in a tiny tea-shop in the village of Mayfield in Sussex.

Metric	US	Imperial	
450g	1lb	1lb	cooking apples, cooked and puréed
			finely grated rind and juice of 2 large lemons, preferably unwaxed/organic
125g	1 stick	4oz	unsalted butter, melted
4	4	4	large eggs, well beaten
450g	2¼ cups	1lb	caster sugar

Put the apple purée, lemon rind and juice into a double boiler or a heatproof basin set over a saucepan of barely simmering water. Take care not to let the bottom of the bowl touch the water. Add the well beaten eggs, sugar and melted butter. Stir the mixture frequently with a wooden or plastic spoon (metal implements can spoil the flavour) for about 20 minutes, or until thick.

Remove the pan from the heat and pour into warm jars. Cover immediately with waxed paper discs and leave until completely cold. Then cover with cellophane, label and store in the refrigerator for up to 6 weeks.

VARIATION

Spicy Apple Curd Add 5ml/1tsp/1tsp of ground cinnamon and ground ginger to the apples when cooking. Proceed as above.

Blackberry Curd

This is delicious spread thickly on drop scones, crusty bread or hot buttered muffins.

Metric	US	Imperial	
350g	12oz	12oz	blackberries
225g	8oz	8oz	cooking apples
			grated rind and juice of 1 large lemon, preferably unwaxed/organic
125g	1 stick	4oz	butter
350g	1¾ cups	12oz	caster sugar
4	4	4	large eggs, well beaten

Wash the blackberries and peel, core and chop the apples. Place in a saucepan and cook gently together for about 15 minutes or until really soft. Rub through a nylon sieve then continue as for Mayfield Apple Curd (see page 98).

VARIATION

Raspberry or Loganberry Curd Substitute raspberries or loganberries for the blackberries.

Gooseberry Curd

This curd has a very subtle flavour and makes a delightful spread for fresh bread and butter. It is also good as a filling for cakes, especially chocolate-flavoured, for tarts and as a topping for cheesecakes.

Metric	US	Imperial	
450g	1lb	1lb	green gooseberries
about 30ml	about 1 tbsp	about 1 tbsp	water
125g	1 stick	4oz	butter
225g	1 cup	8oz	caster sugar
4	4	4	large eggs, well beaten

Wash the gooseberries and top and tail them. Cook gently in a little water for about 15 minutes or until very soft. Rub through a nylon sieve, then continue as for Mayfield Apple Curd, (see page 98).

Strawberry and Orange Curd

This curd makes a mouth-watering filling for a Victoria sandwich with or without cream. If you pick your own strawberries from a farm, this is an ideal recipe for using up any slightly squashed berries at the bottom of the container.

Metric	US	Imperial	
225g	8oz	8oz	strawberries, preferably organic
			finely grated rind and juice of 1 large orange, preferably unwaxed/organic
4	4	4	large eggs, beaten
125g	1 stick	4oz	unsalted butter
225g	1 cup	8oz	caster sugar

Hull the strawberries and make sure that they are clean, but don't wash them. Mash with a fork, then proceed as for Mayfield Apple Curd (see page 98).

Trelissick Lemon Curd

The restaurant at Trelissick make this delicious lemon curd as a filling for their much-loved home-made lemon sponge. They make it in a slow cooker and assure me it also freezes well.

Metric	US	Imperial	
			finely grated rind and juice of 2 large lemons, preferably unwaxed/organic
4	4	4	large eggs, lightly beaten
175g	³/₄ cup	6oz	caster sugar
125g	1 stick	4oz	unsalted butter, melted

Place the lemon rind and juice in a basin or dish that will fit in the slow cooker. Add the beaten eggs, sugar and melted butter and stir well. Cover with a piece of foil and place in the slow cooker. Pour in enough boiling water to come half-way up the basin or dish, then cover with the lid of the slow cooker. Cook for about 1¹/₂–2 hours until thick. Stir well with a wooden spoon, then pot in warm jars.

VARIATIONS

If you do not have a slow cooker, follow the method for Mayfield Apple Curd (see page 98).

Lime Curd Substitute 4 limes for the lemons.

Grapefruit Curd Substitute 1¹/₂ grapefruit for the lemons.

Tangerine Curd Use 2–3 tangerines (depending on size) instead of the lemons and reduce the amount of sugar to 125g/¹/₂ cup/4oz.

Orange Curd Use 1 large orange, preferably Seville or bitter orange when in season, instead of the lemons and reduce the amount of sugar to 125g/¹/₂ cup/4oz.

St Clement's Curd Use 1 medium orange and 1 large lemon instead of the 2 lemons and reduce the amount of sugar to 125g/¹/₂ cup/4oz.

May's Pumpkin Cream

This super recipe was invented by a neighbour of mine in Cornwall, a retired professional cook who worked for a local family. She wanted to find new ways of using pumpkins grown in the kitchen garden and recommends this curd as a filling for pies and tarts, or a spread on scones and muffins.

Metric	US	Imperial	
450g	1lb	1lb	pumpkin, when prepared
30ml	2tbsp	2tbsp	water
2	2	2	large eggs, well beaten
350g	12oz	12oz	caster sugar
			finely grated rind of 1 lemon, preferably unwaxed/organic
			finely grated rind of 1 orange, preferably unwaxed/organic
2·5ml	½tsp	½tsp	ground mace
2·5ml	½tsp	½tsp	ground ginger
			pinch of freshly ground nutmeg

Cut the pumpkin flesh into cubes and place in a pan with the water. Cook over a low heat until tender, then raise the heat to evaporate any surplus liquid. Purée the pumpkin in a food processor or push through a fine nylon sieve. Put the pumpkin purée into a double boiler or a heatproof basin over a saucepan of barely simmering water. Add the beaten eggs, sugar, lemon rind and juice, orange rind and juice and the spices. Continue to cook as for Mayfield Apple Curd (see page 98).

VARIATION

Spicy Marrow Cream Substitute marrow for the pumpkin.

CHAPTER 8

Marmalades and Mincemeats

Marmalades

The term marmalade dates back to the Middle Ages, but was not originally applied to a preserve of citrus fruits. It was, rather, a stiff paste of quinces, honey and spices, cut into small shapes and served as a sweetmeat (see Fruit Pastes, page 96). This confection was a luxury article imported in boxes, usually from Portugal, and was called after the Portuguese for 'quince', *marmelo*. It became subject to high customs duty, so English housewives learned to make their own marmalade from home-grown quinces.

Gradually 'marmalade' was used to describe any fruit cooked to a pulp with sugar or honey and spices and used to fill pies or tarts or eaten as sweetmeats. Citrus fruits were sometimes included. Oranges and lemons first arrived as luxury items in England in the thirteenth century, but from the end of the fourteenth century the shipments became more frequent and prices fell. The oranges were always of the Seville type, coming in from Spain or Portugal or on the spice ships belonging to the Venetians and the Genoese. In addition to citrus fruits, jars of 'citrenade' were imported. This was a kind of 'marmalade' made from lemons – it was solid in texture and eaten in pieces rather than used as a spread.

Sweet oranges were first brought back from Ceylon during the sixteenth century by the Portuguese and soon spread into the orange-growing countries of southern Europe. A century later, a superior fruit with a sweet flavour, the 'China' orange, became so fashionable that a few wealthy garden owners, such as Elizabeth I's chief minister, Lord Burghley, tried to coax orange trees to fruit in the English climate. By the end of the eighteenth century, they, along with lemon, had become the most easily grown exotic fruit with elegant buildings to house the tender trees gracing many a country-house garden. The National Trust owns many fine orangeries – notably at Dyrham Park, near Bath, at Saltram in Devon and Felbrigg and Blickling Halls, which are both in Norfolk.

The first true orange marmalade was probably made in the eighteenth century by the Keiller family in Scotland. It is said that James Keiller, a Dundee grocer, was tempted to buy a large quantity of cheap Spanish oranges, which did not sell well in his shop as they were of the bitter Seville type. He took them home and his wife made them into jam, or the first orange marmalade. She had already established a good trade for her quince preserve known as 'marmalet' and the same customers flocked to buy her new product. With her son she set up a factory to make marmalade, which is still thriving today. However, marmalade was not properly introduced into England until 1870 when a grocer's wife from Oxford, a Mrs Cooper, decided to make a small amount. She was overwhelmed by the demand, and marmalade in time became the standard item on the breakfast table.

Although marmalade is a traditional breakfast preserve, it is excellent in cakes, puddings and tarts. Try it also as a filling with cream for an orange or lemon sponge, or as a flavouring for ice-cream. Marmalade is very good served with cold ham, pork, duck or goose, or used for basting these meats.

Home-made marmalade is not only more delicious, but much cheaper than shop-bought. It can vary from a thick, chunky consistency to a clear sparkling jelly depending on the recipe.

To Make Marmalade

1 Scrub the fruit to remove dirt and chemicals and prepare according to the recipe. If possible, buy unwaxed or organic citrus fruit. (Cut up the fruit by hand if you want the best, most even result, or use a marmalade cutter or food processor.)
2 Simmer the cut peel, uncovered, until the liquid has reduced by half and the peel is very tender. (It will not become any softer after the sugar has been added.)
3 Warmed sugar dissolves faster when added to the simmered peel. Ensure that the sugar has dissolved completely before boiling for a set or it may crystallise later in the preserve.
4 To test for setting, drop a little marmalade on a cold plate. If it wrinkles when pushed with a finger a few minutes later, it will set.
5 Make sure that the jars are spotlessly clean and heat them in a cool oven (60°C/ 120°F) before filling with the marmalade.
6 To prevent the peel rising to the top of the jars, allow the marmalade to stand for ten minutes, then stir it before potting.
7 Packets of jam-pot covers include discs of waxed paper. Put one of these, waxed side down, on the surface of the marmalade as soon as the jar is filled. When it is completely cold, apply the cover. Label and store in a dry, dark, airy cupboard.

Daddy's Seville Orange Marmalade

Bitter oranges are the most popular fruit for marmalade because of their flavour and appearance. The peel of sweet oranges gives marmalade a rather cloudy finish and the pith does not turn as translucent. Unfortunately, Sevilles and other bitter oranges have a very short season – usually just before Christmas to the first week of February. They can be frozen for use later in the year but my father, the 'marmalade king' in our family, thinks that the resultant marmalade is inferior. Here is his recipe which is excellent and frequently wins prizes in our local produce show.

Metric	US	Imperial	
900g	2lb	2lb	bitter oranges, preferably Seville oranges
1	1	1	sweet orange
1	1	1	lemon
2·4 litres	10$\frac{1}{3}$ cups	4 pints	water
1·8kg	6$\frac{1}{2}$ cups	4lb	sugar

Cut all the fruits in half, removing and reserving all the pips. Shred the fruit fairly finely, including the pith. Steep the reserved pips in a small basin with 600ml/2$\frac{1}{2}$ cups/1 pint of the water. Put the shredded fruit in a large bowl and pour in the remaining water. Cover the bowl with a clean cloth and leave the fruit to stand overnight.

Place the fruit and its liquor in a large pan and bring to the boil. Boil for about 2 hours or until the peel is tender. Then strain the water from the pips into the pan of fruit and tie the pips in a piece of muslin.

Add the muslin bag to the pan and gradually stir in the warmed sugar. Heat gently until the sugar has completely dissolved, then increase the heat and bring the mixture back to the boil. Boil rapidly, stirring frequently to prevent burning for about 10-15 minutes, or until setting point is reached. Add a small knob of butter to clear any scum and leave to stand for about 10 minutes. Stir, then pot and cover in the usual way (see page 103).

Grapefruit Marmalade

When Seville oranges are unavailable, this makes a good substitute. Choose thin-skinned grapefruit if possible.

Metric	US	Imperial	
900g	2lb	2lb	grapefruit
450g	1lb	1lb	lemons
3·6 litres	15 cups	6 pints	water
2·75kg	12$\frac{3}{4}$ cups	6lb	sugar

Thinly pare off the rind from the washed fruit with a potato peeler and cut into thin strips. Place in a large pan. Cut all the pith from the fruit with a sharp knife and reserve it. Slice the fruit and add it to the pan with any juice. Tie the pips and reserved pith in a piece of muslin and add to the pan with the water. Bring to the boil, then reduce the heat and simmer gently for 1-1½ hours, or until the peel is very soft and disintegrates when squeezed. Remove the muslin bag, squeezing the juice back into the pan, and discard. Add the warmed sugar and stir over a low heat until dissolved, then boil rapidly, stirring frequently until setting point is reached (start testing after about 10 minutes). Stir in a knob of butter to disperse the scum. Allow the marmalade to cool for about 10 minutes, then stir. Pot and cover the usual way (see page 103).

Peckover Lemon Marmalade

Alexandrina Peckover of Peckover House in Wisbech in Cambridgeshire contributed a recipe for 'Citron Marmalade' to a local WI recipe book in the 1920s. The restaurant at Peckover is now making a marmalade based on this recipe, using lemons instead of citrons.

Metric	US	Imperial	
8	8	8	lemons, roughly chopped
1·7 litres	7½ cups	3 pints	water
1·35kg	5¼ cups	3lb	sugar

Reduce the lemons to a pulp in a food processor. Put into a large bowl with the water. Cover with a clean cloth and leave to soak for 24 hours. Place the fruit and liquid in a large pan and bring to the boil. Boil for 2 hours until the peel is tender. Gradually stir in the warmed sugar making sure that it is completely dissolved before bringing back to the boil. Boil rapidly for about 30 minutes or until setting point is reached (see page 103). Pot and cover in the usual way.

Lime Marmalade

I particularly like this recipe, with its fine shreds of peel in the clear jelly. Limes and grapefruit arrived in Britain later than oranges and lemons. By the 1680s, casks of lime juice were being exported from Jamaica to make punch, a drink newly popular in England. Later, the British Navy, realising that the drinking of lime juice helped to fight scurvy, made it compulsory for their sailors – hence the nickname of 'Limey' for a Briton.

Metric	US	Imperial	
1·35kg	3lb	3lb	limes
3·6 litres	15 cups	6 pints	water
2·75kg	13 cups	6lb	sugar

Pare the rind from the limes with a potato peeler, then cut it into fine shreds. Cut all the pith off the fruit and place in a piece of muslin. Slice the lime flesh, adding the pips to the pith. Tie the muslin into a bag. Place the rind, flesh and muslin bag with the water in a large pan and bring to the boil. Reduce the heat, then simmer for about 1½ hours, or until the lime rind is very soft. Remove the muslin bag, squeezing the juice back into the pan. Add the warmed sugar and stir over a low heat until it has completely dissolved. Bring to the boil and boil rapidly until setting point is reached (see page 103). Stir in a knob of butter to remove any scum and allow to stand for 10 minutes. Pot and cover in the usual way.

VARIATIONS

Ginger Marmalade Follow the above recipe, using demerara sugar. Stir in 125g/ 4oz/4oz preserved stem ginger, finely chopped, with the warmed sugar. Continue as before. Grapefruit also makes a good base for a Ginger Marmalade (see page 104).

Dark Oxford Marmalade This is a chunky, coarse-cut marmalade for true marmalade lovers. Its rich, dark colour is achieved by adding black treacle. Follow the main recipe above, cutting the fruit into thick shreds or chunks. Add 15ml/1tbsp/ 1tbsp black treacle with the sugar.

Dark Oxford Marmalade with Whisky Make as above and stir in about 30ml/ 2tbsp/2tbsp whisky after setting point has been reached.

Seville Jelly Marmalade

My father makes this specially for me as I really prefer a fine jelly marmalade. It is very good served as an accompaniment to cold ham, pork, duck or even pork sausages, as well as being delicious spread thickly on warm, buttered toast. If a completely clear jelly is required, don't remove any peel from the oranges.

Metric	US	Imperial	
900g	2lb	2lb	Seville oranges
1	1	1	sweet orange
2	2	2	lemons
4·2 litres	18 cups	7 pints	water
1·8kg	8½ cups	4lb	sugar (approx. amounts)

Thinly pare the rind from half the Seville oranges if you want some peel suspended in the jelly marmalade. Shred the rind very finely and steep in 300ml/1¼ cups/½ pint water in a large bowl. Cover the chopped fruit with 1·7 litres/7½ cups/3 pints water and leave to steep for 24 hours.

Turn the fruit and steeping liquor into a large pan and add the remaining water. Strain the shredded peel and add its soaking liquor to the pan. Tie the peel in a piece of muslin and add it. Bring the fruit to the boil and boil gently for 1¼ hours. Remove and reserve the muslin bag of shredded peel, gently pressing out excess liquid back into the pan. Continue to cook the fruit for a further 15–45 minutes or until the mixture has reduced by half. Remove the rind from the muslin and rinse in cold water, then drain. Strain the fruit mixture through a jelly-bag and set aside in a covered container. Measure the strained liquid and pour it back into the pan. Add 450g/2½ cups/1lb sugar for each 600ml/2½ cups/1 pint liquid. Add the reserved shredded peel and stir well over a gentle heat until the sugar has dissolved completely.

Increase the heat and bring to the boil. Boil rapidly for about 20 minutes or until setting point is reached. (It is best to start testing for setting point after 15 minutes.) After removing any scum, allow the marmalade to stand for about 10 minutes. Stir gently to distribute the peel evenly then pot and cover as usual (see page 103).

Tangerine Marmalade

Metric	US	Imperial	
900g	2lb	2lb	tangerines
450g	1lb	1lb	lemons
3·6 litres	15 cups	6 pints	water
2·75kg	12¾ cups	6lb	sugar

Cut the fruit in half and squeeze out the juice. Pour the juice into a large pan reserving the pips. Tie the pips in a piece of muslin and add them to the juice. Shred the tangerine and lemon rinds without removing the pith, and add to the pan. Pour in the water and bring to the boil. Reduce the heat, then simmer for about 1½ hours, or until the peel is very soft. Remove the muslin bag, squeezing the juice back into the pan. Add the warmed sugar and stir over a low heat until it has completely dissolved. Bring to the boil, then boil rapidly until setting point is reached (see page 103). Stir in a knob of butter to disperse the scum then allow to cool slightly. Stir to distribute the peel, then pot and cover in the usual way (see page 103).

Three Fruit Marmalade

This is a very useful stand-by recipe, which does not require seasonal Seville oranges. Follow the suggested proportions of different fruit for a good set as the lemons are the main source of pectin, rather than the grapefruit or sweet oranges.

Metric	US	Imperial	
1·35kg	3lb	3lb	mixed citrus fruit (about 2 grapefruit, 2 sweet oranges and 4 lemons)
3·6litres	15cups	6pints	water
2·75kg	12¾cups	6lb	sugar

Cut all the fruit in half, then squeeze out the juice and pour into a large pan. Tie the pips in a piece of muslin and add to the juice in the pan. Cut the orange and lemon rinds in half again and the grapefruit rind into quarters. Slice the pieces of peel into thick or thin shreds, as you prefer, without removing the pith, and add to the pan with the water. Bring to the boil, then reduce the heat and simmer for 1½ hours, or until the peel is very soft.

Remove the muslin bag, squeezing the juice back into the pan. Add the warmed sugar and stir over a low heat until completely dissolved, then bring to the boil and boil rapidly until setting point is reached (see page 103). Add a knob of butter to disperse the scum, then allow to cool slightly before potting and covering in the usual way.

Mincemeats

Until the twentieth century, mincemeat was, as its name suggests, a mixture of minced or shredded meat, dried fruits and spices, and has always been associated with Christmas and other festive occasions. Dried fruits and spices were expensive and therefore a special treat. The original 'minced pye' was oval to represent the manger and contained a pastry baby. Oliver Cromwell banned it in the seventeenth century as being far too rich and indulgent, and hinting of paganism.

Mincemeats can be made from any combination of dried and glacé fruits, nuts and spices, so it is well worth experimenting. To keep well, the mincemeat should not have too high a proportion of apple or fresh ingredients to dried or candied fruits and sugar. The alcohol content and acid in the fruit juice also act as preservatives. Make sure the jars you store the mincemeat in are sterilised as any impurities can cause fermentation. This can also be caused by incorrect storage, so find a cool place, such as an unheated room or a box in the garage. Store in the refrigerator if you have nowhere else suitable. Any opened jars and part-used jars of mincemeat should be placed in the refrigerator and used up quickly.

A traditional method of preventing fermentation is to place the mincemeat, minus the brandy, in a cool oven (60°C/120°F) for 3 hours. Allow it to get completely cold before stirring in the brandy, potting and storing.

Traditional Mincemeat

A seventeenth-century recipe in the Dryden family papers at Canons Ashby included minced ox tongue, beef suet and hard-boiled eggs with the dried fruit, apples, candied peel and spices. Rose- or orange-flower water and a little sack or brandy was used to moisten the mincemeat. A later, eighteenth-century, recipe from Erddig replaces the tongue with meat and omits the egg and flower water. Mrs Scott, who gave the recipe to the Yorke family, recommended using Seville oranges instead of sweet as they give an excellent flavour.

Metric	US	Imperial	
450g	1lb	1lb	eating apples
125g	³/₄ cup	4oz	unblanched almonds
450g	3 cups	1lb	raisins
175g	1 cup	6oz	sultanas
175g	1 cup	6oz	currants
50g	2oz	2oz	mixed candied citron and lemon peel
50g	2oz	2oz	candied orange peel
125g	4oz	4oz	beef or vegetable suet
450g	2¼ cups	1lb	soft brown sugar
			grated rind and juice of 2 lemons, preferably unwaxed/organic
			grated rind and juice of 2 sweet or Seville oranges, preferably unwaxed/organic
10ml	2 tsp	2 tsp	ground mixed spice
10ml	2 tsp	2 tsp	ground cinnamon
2·5ml	½ tsp	½ tsp	freshly grated nutmeg
150ml	²/₃ cup	¼ pint	brandy

Peel, core and finely chop, or grate the apples. Place the almonds in a basin and cover with boiling water. Leave for 5 minutes, then drain and slip off the skins. Place immediately in cold water, leave for a few minutes, then chop finely. Place all the ingredients, except the brandy, in a large bowl and stir well. Cover with a clean cloth and leave for 2 days in a cool place to allow the flavours to develop. Stir again very thoroughly, then stir in the brandy. Pack the mincemeat into sterilised jars and cover with clean lids or cellophane jam pot covers. Label and store for at least 1 month before using, to allow the flavours to mature. Use within 3 months.

Apricot and Hazelnut Mincemeat

If you dislike candied peel, this is the recipe for you. Dried figs make a delicious alternative to the dates if you want to experiment.

Metric	US	Imperial	
450g	1lb	1lb	cooking apples
225g	1½ cups	8oz	large raisins, stoned
225g	8oz	8oz	dates, stoned
450g	1lb	1lb	dried apricots
450g	3 cups	1lb	sultanas
125g	4oz	4oz	glacé cherries, washed
50g	2oz	2oz	candied angelica
125g	scant 1 cup	4oz	hazelnuts
50g	2oz	2oz	crystallised ginger
225g	8oz	8oz	beef suet, shredded or vegetable suet
350g	2 cups	12oz	soft dark brown sugar
			grated rind and juice of 1 lemon, preferably unwaxed/organic
			grated rind and juice of 1 orange, preferably unwaxed/organic
5ml	1tsp	1tsp	ground mixed spice
5ml	1tsp	1tsp	ground cinnamon
5ml	1tsp	1tsp	ground mace
150ml	⅔ cup	¼ pint	brandy

Peel, core and finely chop or grate the apples. Finely chop the dates, apricots, glacé cherries, angelica, hazelnuts and crystallised ginger. Mix all the ingredients together in a large bowl, cover with a clean cloth and leave to stand overnight. Stir again, then pot in sterilised jars. Cover and store for at least 3 months before using to allow the flavours to mature.

Mincemeat Cooked in Cider

This recipe contains no suet and yet is full of fruity richness. A larger proportion of apples is used, as well as glacé cherries, and the mincemeat is cooked. Cider as well as rum is included, but you can alter this as you like. This mincemeat keeps extremely well.

Metric	US	Imperial	
400ml	1½ cups	¾ pint	medium cider
450g	2¼ cups	1lb	soft dark brown sugar
1·8kg	4lb	4lb	cooking apples
450g	1lb	1lb	currants
450g	3 cups	1lb	raisins
125g	4oz	4oz	glacé cherries, chopped
125g	1 cup	4oz	blanched almonds, chopped
			grated rind and juice of 1 lemon, preferably unwaxed/organic
5ml	1tsp	1tsp	ground mixed spice
5ml	1tsp	1tsp	ground cinnamon
2·5ml	½tsp	½tsp	ground cloves
30ml	2tbsp	2tbsp	rum

Place the cider and sugar in a large pan and heat gently, stirring occasionally, until the sugar has dissolved. Peel, core and roughly chop apples. Add to the pan, and stir in all the remaining ingredients except the rum. Bring the mixture slowly to the boil, stirring all the time. Reduce the heat, half-cover with a lid and simmer gently for about 30 minutes or until the mixture has become a soft pulp, stirring occasionally. Test for sweetness, adding more sugar if necessary. Remove from the heat and set aside until completely cold. Stir in the rum, then pack into sterilised jars, cover and store.

Cherry and Walnut Mincemeat

Metric	US	Imperial	
about 900g	about 2lb	about 2lb	Bramley apples, peeled, cored, cooked and puréed (see method)
1kg	2¼lb	2¼lb	mixed dried fruit
225g	8oz	8oz	glacé cherries
125g	4oz	4oz	whole candied peel
125g	scant 1 cup	4oz	walnuts
2·5ml	½tsp	½tsp	freshly grated nutmeg
5ml	1tsp	1tsp	ground cinnamon
			grated rind and juice of 1 lemon, preferably unwaxed/organic
			grated rind and juice of 1 orange, preferably unwaxed/organic
15ml	1tbsp	1tbsp	ground mixed spice
225g	1 cup	8oz	muscovado sugar
60ml	¼ cup	4tbsp	brandy, sweet sherry or port

This unusual mincemeat does not contain suet.

You will need 675g/1½lb/1½lb cooked apple purée: reserve any additional purée for another use.

Coarsely chop the mixed fruit, cherries and peel. Finely chop the walnuts. Place all the ingredients in a large bowl. Cover with a clean cloth and leave overnight. Pack the mixture into sterilised jars, cover and store for up to 6 weeks.

Pear and Fig Mincemeat

This recipe uses pears instead of apples as its base. You can substitute dates for the figs if you prefer, and walnuts for the almonds. Sherry, rum, whisky or cider can be used instead of brandy.

Metric	US	Imperial	
900g	2lb	2lb	cooking pears
450g	3 cups	1lb	raisins
450g	3 cups	1lb	sultanas
225g	1²/₃ cups	8oz	currants
225g	8oz	8oz	dried figs
125g	4oz	4oz	whole candied orange peel
125g	4oz	4oz	mixed, whole candied lemon and citron peel
225g	1 cup	8oz	blanched almonds
450g	2¼ cups	1lb	demerara sugar
450g	1lb	1lb	beef or vegetable suet
			grated rind and juice of 2 lemons, preferably unwaxed/organic
10ml	2tsp	2tsp	ground mixed spice
5ml	1tsp	1tsp	ground ginger
5ml	1tsp	1tsp	ground cinnamon
2·5ml	½tsp	½tsp	freshly grated nutmeg
150ml	²/₃ cup	¼ pint	brandy

Peel, core and finely chop or grate the pears. Chop the other fruit, peel and nuts. Place all the ingredients in a large china bowl. Cover with a clean cloth and leave to stand for 2 or 3 days. Stir the mincemeat thoroughly, then pack into sterilised jars, cover and store.

Freezer Mincemeat

Metric	US	Imperial	
675g	1½lb	1½lb	cooking apples, peeled, cored and finely chopped
225g	⅔ cup	8oz	currants
225g	1½ cups	8oz	sultanas
225g	1½ cups	8oz	seedless raisins
125g	4oz	4oz	mixed whole citron and lemon candied peel
125g	4oz	4oz	whole orange candied peel
			grated rind and juice of 1 lemon, preferably unwaxed/organic
75g	½ cup	3oz	blanched almonds
450g	2¼ cups	1lb	soft dark brown sugar
125g	4oz	4oz	beef or vegetable suet
5ml	1 tsp	1 tsp	ground cinnamon
5ml	1 tsp	1 tsp	freshly grated nutmeg
			grated rind of 1 orange, preferably unwaxed/organic

Blanch the apples in boiling water for 30 seconds, then drain very thoroughly in a colander and cool. Place the cooled apples in a large bowl. Chop the dried fruit, peel nuts and add to the apples. Stir thoroughly, then ladle the mixture into plastic containers and freeze for up to 4 months. Thaw overnight in the refrigerator, then add brandy or sherry before using.

CHAPTER 9

Candied, Crystallised and Glacé Fruits, Nuts and Flowers

The art of candying and working with sugar was invented in Italy, but practised widely in Tudor and Stuart England. General cookery books began to offer recipes for sweetmeats and candied produce and soon separate handbooks appeared with titles such as *Delights for Ladies* written by Sir Hugh Platt in 1605. They were meant for the lady of the house, as it was she, not the cook and kitchen staff, who was responsible for making 'banqueting stuff' for the final or 'banquet' course of a meal. Candied fruit, wild plants, flowers and vegetables were all eaten at the banquet.

The candying process consists of covering the chosen produce with a hot syrup, then gradually increasing the sugar content of the syrup day by day, until it becomes really heavy and the produce is impregnated with sugar. It is important to do this slowly, in stages, to give the sugar time to penetrate as water is extracted. If candying is rushed, the produce will become tough and shrivelled.

Nowadays we tend to eat candied or crystallised fruits only at Christmas time, but they make a really delicious and impressive end to a special meal throughout the year. They also make lovely presents. They are perhaps in the luxury class, but are much cheaper when made at home.

Apricots, pears, pineapple, cherries and figs are among the most successful fruits for candying as they have a pronounced flavour. Plums, greengages, crab apples and peaches may also be used. Do not mix different varieties of fruit in the same syrup because the individual flavours will be lost.

Fruit for candying should be of good quality and fully ripe but still firm, so that its flavour is at its peak. If you are cutting up the fruit, make the pieces more or less the same size. Place the prepared fruit in sufficient boiling water to cover and cook gently until just tender. Overcooking spoils the shape and texture, while undercooking causes slow penetration of the syrup and results in a dark colour and tough texture. Whereas soft fruit may only need 2–4 minutes cooking, tough fruit may take 10–15 minutes. Drain the cooked fruit, reserving the liquid to make the syrup. Granulated sugar is generally recommended for the syrup but glucose may be substituted for some of the sugar.

The candying will take 2–3 weeks depending on how sweet you like candied fruit to be. Any left-over syrup can be added to fresh fruit salad or used as a sauce to serve with ice-cream, sponge puddings or milk puddings.

Candied Apricots

Plums, greengages, small tangerines, cherries and crab apples can be candied whole in the same way as apricots.

Metric	US	Imperial	
450g	1lb	1lb	fresh apricots
675g	2³⁄₄ cups	1¹⁄₂lb	sugar
			For glacé finish
450g	2¹⁄₄ cups	1lb	sugar
150ml	²⁄₃ cup	¹⁄₄ pint	water

Prick the apricots all over with a stainless steel or silver fork. Put them in a pan and pour on enough boiling water to cover. Cook very gently for 10-15 minutes or until just tender. Drain the apricots, reserving 300ml/1¹⁄₄ cup/¹⁄₂pint of the cooking liquid. Put the fruit in a basin.

Return the liquid to the pan and add 175g/1 cup/6oz sugar. Heat gently until the sugar has completely dissolved, then bring to the boil and pour over the apricots. Leave for 24 hours.

Drain off the syrup into a pan, add 50g/¹⁄₄ cup/2oz sugar and heat gently until it has dissolved. Bring to the boil, then pour the syrup over the apricots and leave to soak for 24 hours. Repeat this 5 times, adding 50g/¹⁄₄ cup/2oz sugar each time, and leave the fruit to soak for a full 24 hours each time.

On the following day (day 8), repeat the process, adding 75g/¹⁄₃ cup/3oz sugar to the syrup. Add the apricots and simmer for 3-4 minutes. Return the apricots and the syrup to the basin and leave to soak for a further 48 hours. Finally, repeat the process adding a further 75g/¹⁄₃ cup/3oz sugar to the syrup and leave the fruit to soak for 4 days.

Drain the apricots, put them on a wire rack and dry in a very cool oven 60°C/120°F, or in a warm cupboard until the surface of the fruit is no longer sticky. Turn the apricots 2 or 3 times during the drying process, which may take up to 3 days.

To give the apricots a glacé finish, prepare a fresh syrup by dissolving 450g/ 2¹⁄₄ cups/1lb sugar in a 150ml/²⁄₃ cup/¹⁄₄ pint water over a gentle heat. When the sugar has dissolved, bring the syrup to the boil and boil rapidly for 1 minute. Pour a little of this syrup into a hot cup. Cover the rest of the syrup in the pan with a damp cloth and keep it warm (a double boiler is good for this). Using a skewer or fork, dip each apricot into boiling water for 20 seconds, then quickly into the syrup.

Place the dipped apricots on a wire rack to dry. As the syrup in the cup becomes cloudy, replace it with a fresh batch from the pan. When the apricots are dipped, place them in a warm place, turning them occasionally until they are dry. Fruits with this glacé finish retain more moisture and are therefore juicier than other candied fruit. When the apricots are thoroughly dried, pack them in cardboard or wooden boxes between layers of waxed paper.

To use glucose as well as sugar, when first making the syrup with the water from cooking the fruit, reduce the quantity of sugar to 50g/¼ cup/2oz sugar and add 125g/4oz/4oz glucose.

Crystallised Orange Segments and Grapes

Oranges and grapes do not need cooking before they are candied. In this case, they can be candied together using the same syrup. The orange segments can be dipped in plain chocolate to make a delicious sweetmeat to serve with coffee. Large tangerines or clementines may be used instead of oranges.

Metric	US	Imperial	
2-3	2-3	2-3	small oranges
225g	8oz	8oz	black or green grapes
300ml	1¼ cups	½ pint	water
575g	2½ cups	1¼ lb	sugar
			caster sugar to finish
			plain chocolate to coat

Remove the peel and pith from the oranges and divide carefully into segments, taking care to avoid breaking the fine membrane around each segment. Weigh the prepared oranges – you need 225g/8oz/8oz. Remove the grapes from their stalks and remove their pips if necessary. Together the fruit should weigh 450g/1lb/1lb. Place the fruit in a shallow dish. Make a sugar syrup by dissolving 175g/1 cup/6oz sugar in 300ml/ 1¼ cups/½ pint water in a saucepan over a very gentle heat. When the sugar has dissolved completely, bring the syrup to the boil and boil rapidly for 1 minute. Pour the warm syrup over the fruit. Cover and leave for 24 hours.

Drain off the syrup and reboil, adding another 50g/¼ cup/2oz sugar. Pour over the fruit again and leave for a further 24 hours. Repeat this process 3 more times, adding 50g/¼ cup/2oz extra sugar to the syrup and leaving for 24 hours each time. Drain the syrup again, return it to the pan, adding 75g/⅓ cup/3oz sugar this time and bring to the boil. Add the fruit and keep boiling for 3 minutes. Pour the fruit and syrup back into the dish and leave for 24 hours. Repeat the boiling process with another 75g/⅓ cup/3oz. Thoroughly drain the fruit and place it on a wire rack. Dry until crisp in a very cool oven 60°C/120°F or in a warm airing cupboard. When the fruit is completely dry, dip each piece quickly into boiling water, shake off excess moisture and then roll it in caster sugar. Leave to dry again. Melt the chocolate in a bowl over hot water, then dip the orange segments to half-coat them. Place on non-stick baking parchment until the chocolate has set. Pack between layers of waxed paper in cardboard or wooden boxes.

Crystallised Pears

Peaches, figs and pineapple rings can be crystallised in the same way as pears.

Metric	US	Imperial	
450g	1lb	1lb	pears
675g	2³/₄ cups	1¹/₂lb	granulated sugar
			caster sugar to finish

Peel, core and halve or quarter the pears. Place in a pan and add sufficient boiling water to cover the fruit. Cook very gently for about 10 minutes or until the pears are just tender. Drain the pears and place in a bowl, reserving 300ml/1¹/₄ cups/¹/₂ pint of the cooking liquor. Put this in a pan and follow the method for making Candied Apricots (see page 115).

Instead of applying a glacé finish, give pears a crystallised finish. Using cooking tongs, dip a piece of candied pear quickly into boiling water. Shake off the excess moisture, then roll the fruit in caster sugar. Repeat until all the pieces of pear are coated. Allow to dry thoroughly before packing.

Candied Peel

Home-made candied peel is juicier than the bought variety and has a much better flavour. The peel of oranges, lemons, grapefruit and limes can be candied, but each type should be processed separately to give the best flavour. The following recipe is for candied lemon peel, but the other citrus fruits can be prepared in exactly the same way. The peel can be collected and frozen until you have enough for a boiling. With grapefruit peel, the water should be changed 2 or 3 times during the initial cooking process.

Metric	US	Imperial	
4	4	4	medium oranges or large lemons, preferably unwaxed/organic
125g	³/₄ cup	4oz	glucose
225g	1 cup	8oz	sugar

Wash the fruit thoroughly, then score the peel into quarters and carefully remove it in neat segments. Place in a stainless steel or enamel pan with enough water just to cover. Bring to the boil, then reduce the heat and simmer gently for about 1 hour, or until the peel is very tender, adding more water if necessary. Drain well, reserving the cooking liquor. Make this up to 300ml/1¹/₄ cups/¹/₂ pint water if necessary, and pour into a pan. Add the glucose and half the sugar, dissolve over a low heat, then bring to the boil. Pour the syrup over the peel and leave to stand for 2 days.

Strain off the syrup and add a further 125g/½ cup/4oz sugar. Dissolve this over a gentle heat, bring to the boil and add the peel. Simmer until the peel looks translucent. It can be left in this thick syrup for 2–3 weeks, so you can complete the process at your convenience.

Drain the peel and place it on a wire rack. Any remaining syrup can be poured into the hollows of the lemon peel. Cover and leave to dry in a warm place – a very cool oven or the airing cupboard. Store as for the candied fruit.

VARIATION

Chocolate-dipped Candied Peel To make a delicious after-dinner sweet or special gift, cut candied orange peel into narrow strips and dip both ends into melted chocolate (use best quality, dark bitter chocolate). Allow the chocolate to set before storing the peel as for candied fruit.

Candied Angelica

Angelica is a plant rather than a fruit, but I have included this recipe because it is so easy and much cheaper and far better than shop-bought angelica. The cultivated garden variety of angelica has a better flavour and should be used for candying. The stalks should be picked when young and green in April or early May. When candied they are invaluable for decorating and flavouring cakes, biscuits and puddings.

young angelica stems
caster sugar

Cut selected stems into 7·5cm/3in lengths and cook in boiling water for about 7 minutes until tender. Drain well and scrape off any tough outer skin, (with young angelica this is not usually necessary). Weigh the angelica and layer it in a dish with an equal weight of caster sugar. Cover and set aside for 1–2 days until the sugar has dissolved. Transfer to a pan and heat gently until the syrup has almost evaporated.

Place the pieces of angelica on a wire rack over a plate and leave in a warm place until dry (the airing cupboard or the warming oven of an Aga is ideal). Store in a wooden or cardboard box lined with waxed paper.

Glacé Fruits

These are splendid served as an after-dinner confection or given as a special gift. They cannot be kept for more than a week. Choose a selection of small whole fruits such as kumquats, cherries, grapes, physalis (Chinese gooseberries) and strawberries, or segments of orange, tangerine or lime.

Metric	US	Imperial	
			fruit of your choice
225g	1 cup	8oz	sugar
150ml	²/₃ cup	¼ pint	water
10ml	2 tsp	2 tsp	glucose or a pinch of cream of tartar

Pick over the fruit, making sure that it is ripe and quite dry. Dissolve the sugar in the water, then bring to the boil and add the glucose. If using cream of tartar, dissolve it in a little water before adding to the syrup. Boil rapidly to 154°C/310°F – the hard crack stage. If you do not have a sugar thermometer, you can test the mixture by dropping a small amount into a cup of cold water: if it has boiled long enough, it will become hard. The syrup must not boil beyond this stage and turn colour to caramel. Stop the boiling by dipping the bottom of the pan briefly in cold water.

Have an oiled plate ready and when the syrup has stopped bubbling, use a cocktail stick to spear and dip each fruit in it. Place the coated fruit on the plate and leave to set. When hard, arrange in small paper cases for serving.

Candied Chestnuts

Sweet chestnuts collected on a country walk, plus sugar and patience, make an elegant finale to a dinner party. This recipe does not give quite the same result as the expensive 'marrons glacés', even so, when prettily packed, the chestnuts would make impressive Christmas presents for your friends. Use only the best quality, pure variety, not a synthetic flavouring.

Metric	US	Imperial	
600g	1lb 5oz	1lb 5oz	fresh chestnuts, peeled
			water to cover
225g	1 cup	8oz	glucose
225g	1 cup	8oz	sugar
			a few drops of pure vanilla essence (optional)

Put the chestnuts into a large pan and add enough water to cover. Bring to the boil, then reduce the heat and simmer for about 20 minutes or until just tender. Take care not to overcook as they break up during the candying process. Drain well, reserving 150ml/²/₃ cup/¼ pint of the cooking liquor. Pour this into a pan, add the glucose and sugar (or you can use 450g/1lb sugar) and stir over a gentle heat until dissolved. Add the chestnuts and bring to the boil, remove from the heat, cover and leave to soak for 24 hours in a warm place – an airing cupboard is ideal.

Next day, uncover the pan and bring the syrup back to the boil. Remove from the heat and leave to soak for another 24 hours in a warm place. Repeat this process on the next day, adding vanilla essence before boiling, then remove the pan from the heat, using a slotted spoon, transfer the chestnuts to a wire rack placed over a tray. Leave to dry in a warm place for 2–3 days until the chestnuts are no longer sticky. Pack the Candied Chestnuts as for Candied Apricots (see page 115). They are ready to eat immediately and should be eaten within 6 months.

VARIATION

Instead of drying the chestnuts after candying, you can store them in their syrup for 3–4 weeks in a covered container in the refrigerator.

Crystallised Flowers

The English enthusiasm for crystallised flowers, with their pretty appearance and sweet taste, dates back to Elizabethan and Stuart times. They were added to salads, used to decorate jellies and elaborate creamy desserts, and served as sweetmeats at the end of a meal. The most popular flowers for crystallising then were pot marigolds, borage, violets, daisies, cowslips, primroses and, best loved of all, the rose.

Crystallising, or frosting, is a simple and effective way of preventing edible flowers from wilting and preserving the bloom for later use. Although the process is rather time-consuming, it is very simple and utterly addictive!

Provided that the plants are free from pesticide sprays, a great variety of flowers are edible. As a general rule, avoid any flower that comes from a bulb to ensure you do not consume a poisonous plant. If you are in any doubt about whether a flower is edible, check with an expert source.

Choose flowers with a clear bright colour and a flattish shape. (Bell-shaped flowers tend to flatten and lose their shape under the weight of the sugar.) Flowers with large heads, such as roses, carnations, dahlias, mallow and hollyhocks, are more elegant if the petals are removed and crystallised individually. Blossom such as elder, honey-suckle and geranium, which are extremely fragile, are best left intact and then gently broken into florets after frosting.

The flowers of most herbs taste delightful with a delicate flavour of the herb itself. I recommend bergamot, borage, chamomile, chive, lavender, marjoram, mint, pine-apple sage, rocket, rosemary, sage, salad burnet, sorrel, sweet cicely and thyme. The gum arabic method is best as herb flowers are small.

Crystallised Sweet Violets

Choose large, bright purple blooms; the tiny, pale-coloured violets are not as successful. This method of crystallising uses gum arabic and rose-water or orange-flower water. Gum arabic powder can be obtained from any good chemist or cake-decorating suppliers; the scented waters are also sold in supermarkets. Some other suitable edible garden flowers not already mentioned are alyssum, begonia, chrysanthemum, clover, cornflower, forget-me-not, primrose, hawthorn, hibiscus, hops, jasmine, lilac, lime, nasturtium, pansy, pink, sedum and stock.

Metric	US	Imperial	
5ml	1tsp	1tsp	gum arabic powder
15ml	1tbsp	1tbsp	rose- or orange-flower water
			freshly gathered violets
			caster sugar to finish

Put the gum arabic into a small, screw-topped jar and pour on the rose- or orange-flower water. Put on the lid and leave to soak for at least 24 hours, shaking occasionally, until the mixture forms a sticky glue.

Pick the violets on a dry, sunny day when the dew has dried. The flowers must be clean and free from dust. Cover a wire rack with greaseproof paper or muslin and have a plate ready for catching excess sugar as you coat the flowers. Using a small paint brush, paint a violet with gum arabic solution. Coat each petal completely, both back and front, as any areas left unpainted will shrivel and will not keep. Hold the flower over the plate and dredge it lightly all over with caster sugar. Snip off all the stalk and place the flower on the covered rack and leave to dry in a warm place (an airing cupboard is ideal) for 24 hours. Gently move the flowers occasionally to prevent them from sticking to the paper or muslin.

Crystallised violets should be stored in boxes or tins between layers of waxed paper and kept in a cool, dry place. They make a very pretty, old-fashioned decoration for iced cakes, trifles, creamy puddings such as fruit, fools, ice-creams and, of course, for home-made chocolates and Easter eggs.

Crystallised Rose Petals

Full-blown roses can be crystallised as a whole flower, but usually it is easier to treat each petal separately. This recipe gives the alternative way of crystallising flowers and leaves involving egg white and sugar. Personally, I don't find this method as success-ful as gum arabic, but it is fine if you are planning to use the crystallised flowers fairly soon after drying. Choose roses that are a deep pink, red or orange. They add a touch of summer to any dish.

rose petals
1 egg white
caster sugar to finish

Pick roses on a dry, sunny day after the dew has dried. Gently break up each rose into individual petals and, using a fine paint brush, paint petals with lightly beaten egg white. Coat both back and front of the petals and dredge lightly on both sides with caster sugar. Place on a wire rack covered with grease-proof paper and dry in the airing cupboard for 24 hours. Store as for Crystallised Violets and use to decorate junkets, mousses, trifles, cheesecakes and iced sponges.

Sugar-frosted Rosemary

Sprigs of herbs can also be crystallised as well as their flowers (see page 120) and herbs with tiny flowers, of which rosemary is a good example, can be processed when in bloom. Crystallised herb sprigs, such as lemon balm and lemon verbena, make pretty decorations for summer drinks, desserts and cakes. I chose rosemary for this recipe because its use can be traced back to Stuart times. According to John Murrell in *Closet for Ladies* published in 1617: 'To rough-candy sprigs of rosemary. Lay your rosemary branches one by one upon a fair sheet of paper, then take sugar-candy beaten small like sparks of diamonds, and wet it with a little rosewater in a silver spoon, and lay it as even as you can upon every branch.' The sprigs were dried slowly, candied on the other side and could be kept for a year. 'They will appear to the eye in their natural colour, and seen to be covered with sparks of diamonds.'

Metric	US	Imperial	
			small sprigs of fresh rosemary
5ml	1tsp	1tsp	gum arabic powder
15ml	1tbsp	1tbsp	rose-water
			caster sugar to finish

Gather tender sprigs of rosemary from the tips of branches on a dry, sunny day after the dew has dried. Follow the recipe for Crystallised Violets (see page 121). Use to decorate syllabubs, jellies, ice-creams and other creamy puddings.

CHAPTER 10

Fruits Preserved in Alcohol

Bottling fruits in alcohol is one of the oldest, simplest and most delicious ways of preserving them. The luxury fruits grown in the eighteenth century, such as nectarines, peaches, apricots, cherries and grapes, were originally known as 'brandy fruits' because they were preserved in brandy and a little sugar syrup in stone jars ready for the dessert course, when they were usually served in sweetmeat glasses. These preserves make the most luxurious desserts for a special occasion – traditionally at Christmas – and very acceptable presents, especially when packed in attractive airtight jars with decorative labels.

Making Fruits in Alcohol

1 Fruits must be just ripe; if over-ripe they will not retain their shape in the alcohol.
2 Pick over the fruit, removing any damaged or mouldy parts. Wash and dry the fruit and remove the stones, pips, peel and cores as necessary.
3 Soft fruit, such as berries, blackcurrants, apricots and peaches can be used raw, while firmer ones such as apples and hard plums, may require light cooking first.
4 Pack the fruits into sterilised jars (see introduction), either in layers with sugar or in a sugar syrup. Warm the jars if the ingredients used are hot. While granulated sugar is the usual choice of sweetener, brown sugar can be used for flavour, or if a darker colour is preferred.
5 Pour the chosen alcohol over the fruit to cover them completely, making sure that there are no air pockets between them. (The amount of alcohol can vary, depending on the size of the fruits and the amount of sugar used.)
6 Spices such as cloves, cinnamon sticks and allspice berries can be added to the fruits for extra flavour.
7 Seal the jars tightly and leave the fruits in a cool dark place for at least 1 month before using, to allow the flavours to develop. Shake the jars from time to time to blend and dissolve the sugar and flavourings.

As long as the fruits are covered by the alcohol they should keep for about 1 year, and the flavour will improve over this time.

Black Cherries with Port

The aristocrats of the traditional English fruit garden were the wall-trained fruit – the peaches, apricots and cherries. Try using Kirsch, brandy, rum or Amaretto for a change in this recipe. When they have matured for 1 month, the cherries can be decanted into pretty jars if you are giving them as presents.

Metric	US	Imperial	
675g	1¹/₂lb	1¹/₂lb	black cherries
225g	1 cup	8oz	sugar
			port to cover

Wash and dry the cherries and stone them if you wish. Prick them all over with a sterilised darning needle. This allows the port to permeate the skins and flesh, preventing the cherries from shrivelling. Layer the cherries and sugar in sterilised preserving jars filling them to 2·5cm/1in below the rim. Pour in port to cover, then seal the jars. Store in a cool dark place for at least 1 month, moving gently.

Dried Apricots in Eau-de-Vie

This recipe works equally well with fresh or dried cherries, dried pears or with Muscatel raisins.

Metric	US	Imperial	
450g	1lb	1lb	good quality ready-to-eat dried apricots
300ml	1¹/₄ cups	¹/₂ pint	cold water
225g	1 cup	8oz	sugar
3	3	3	sprigs of fresh lemon verbena
about 300ml	about 1¹/₄ cups	about ¹/₂ pint	eau-de-vie

Remove any stalks and leaves from the apricots, then place in a 1 litre/1 quart/2 pint sterilised preserving jar – the fruit should fill just over half the jar. Place the water and sugar in a pan and stir over gentle heat, until the sugar has dissolved. Bring to the boil, then simmer for 5 minutes. Add the lemon verbena sprigs to the apricots, then pour in the hot sugar syrup. Pour in enough eau-de-vie to come to the rim of the jar, making sure that the fruit is covered. Seal the jar tightly and label, then leave in a cold, dark place for 4–8 weeks before eating.

Spiced Fruit and Walnut Compôte in Calvados

Metric	US	Imperial	
225g	1 cup	8oz	caster sugar
6	6	6	firm ripe pears, peeled and cored
4	4	4	whole cloves
1	1	1	bay leaf
1	1	1	cinnamon stick
1	1	1	vanilla pod, split
1	1	1	star anise
5	5	5	black peppercorns
2·5ml	½ tsp	½ tsp	coriander seeds
450g	1 lb	1 lb	dried prunes
225g	1½ cups	8oz	mixed dried fruit, such as apricots, apples & figs
125g	1 cup	4oz	walnut halves (optional)

Quarter or halve the pears depending on size. Put them in a saucepan with the sugar and spices and enough water to just cover the fruit. Cover the saucepan with a lid and heat gently, stirring, until all the sugar has dissolved. Simmer very gently for 10–15 minutes, or until the pears are tender. Remove from the heat, add the prunes, dried fruits and nuts, then leave to cool. Using a slotted spoon remove the fruit and nuts from the syrup. Boil the reserved syrup over a high heat until it has thickened and reduced to 300ml / 1¼ cups / ½ pint. Pour over the fruit, then pour in enough calvados to come to within 2·5cm / 1in of the tops of the jars. Seal and label, then keep in a cool dark place for at least 1 month before using.

Oranges in Brandy

The brandy need not be of the best quality, but do not be tempted to use very cheap brandy either. Try satsumas, tangerines or mandarins instead of oranges. Kumquats can also be used, but should be left whole and pierced all over with a clean darning needle to allow the brandy to penetrate the flesh. Experiment with different liqueurs and spirits, such as Cointreau, Kirsch or rum, if you wish.

Metric	US	Imperial	
12	12	12	small oranges
350g	1¾ cups	12oz	white sugar
300ml	1¼ cups	½ pint	water
5ml	2tsp	2tsp	allspice berries
225ml	¾ cup	7floz	brandy

Using a potato peeler, peel the rind very thinly from 3 of the oranges, taking care to avoid the white pith. Cut the rind into fine strips and blanch in boiling water for 30 seconds, then drain and leave to cool. Cut off the peel and pith from the other 9 oranges and discard. Put 175g/1 cup/6oz sugar and the water in a wide, shallow pan and heat gently, stirring until all the sugar is dissolved. Add the oranges and allspice berries and poach for 5 minutes, turning once.

Spoon the oranges into a colander placed over a smaller pan and leave to drain for 10 minutes, then put on one side to get completely cold. Pour the rest of the poaching syrup into the small pan and add the remaining sugar. Stir over a low heat until the sugar has completely dissolved, then boil rapidly until the temperature rises to 110°C/230°F on a sugar thermometer. Remove the pan from the heat and pour the syrup into a measuring jug (the amount should be equal to the quantity of brandy). Leave to get completely cold, then stir in the brandy.

Pack the oranges into sterilised preserving jars, filling them almost to the top. Add the reserved orange rind to the syrup, then pour over the fruit to cover completely. Seal with air-tight, acid-proof screw tops. Label and store in a cool, dark place for at least 2 months before using.

Apricots in Amaretto

As well as supporting fan-trained fruit, the walls of old kitchen gardens were built as 'hot walls', with flues at intervals to ripen apricots and peaches and to protect the blossom from late frosts. Such walls can be seen in the delightful walled garden at Greys Court near Henley-on-Thames in Oxfordshire and at Westbury Court in Gloucestershire. Peaches or nectarines may be used instead of apricots in this recipe.

Metric	US	Imperial	
1 kg	2¼ lb	2¼ lb	apricots
350g	2 cups	12oz	sugar
600ml	2½ cups	1 pint	amaretto

Prick the apricots all over with a sterilised darning needle and pack them into sterilised preserving jars, layering them with the sugar. Leave 2·5cm / 1in at the top of the jars. Pour the amaretto into the jars to cover the apricots by 1·25cm / ½in, making sure there are no pockets between the fruits. Cover with airtight lids and label. Shake the jars well so that the sugar can start to blend and dissolve in the alcohol. Keep in a cool dark place for at least 2 months before using to allow the flavours to develop. Shake from time to time during the first week of storage to make sure all the sugar dissolves in the alcohol.

Damsons in Mulled Wine

These make a delicious dessert, especially at Christmas.

Metric	US	Imperial	
1 × 75cl	1 × 75cl	1 × 75cl	bottle red wine
4	4	4	whole cloves
6	6	6	cardamon pods, crushed
2	2	2	cinnamon sticks
225g	1 cup	8oz	sugar
900g	2lb	2lb	damsons

Pour the red wine into a saucepan and add the spices and sugar. Heat gently, stirring until the sugar has completely dissolved, then bring to the boil. Reduce the heat and simmer for 20 minutes.

Prick the damsons all over with a sterilised darning needle, then add to the wine mixture. Simmer very gently for about 10 minutes or until the damsons are tender. Remove the pan from the heat and allow to cool. Using a slotted spoon, pack the damsons into sterilised preserving jars. Strain the wine syrup and pour it over the damsons to cover them by 2·5cm / 1in. Seal the jars and label. Keep in a cool dark place for 1 month before using to allow the flavours to develop, but use within 3 months.

CHAPTER 11

Fruit and Flower Drinks

For centuries, fruit, herb and flower-flavoured drinks have been made for both pleasure and for reasons of health. King Henry III is said to have enjoyed wine flavoured with scented flowers, while his son, Edward I, had a taste for sage wine.

In the seventeenth century, ale flavoured with elderberries was drunk in preference to port, and raspberry juice was added to wine to make the popular raspberry sack. Citrus fruit juice, known for its protection against scurvy, was mixed with sack or brandy to make the first lemonade and orangeade.

The eighteenth- and nineteenth-century 'compleat housewife' had to be able to produce numerous waters, ratafias and cordials from spirit flavoured with red roses, poppy petals and the leaves and flowers of rosemary, marjoram and lavender; with fruits like cherries and raspberries and with nuts, such as almonds and apricot kernels.

Sloe Gin

This warming tipple is easy to make, using the fruit of the blackthorn, one of the wild ancestors of our many varieties of cultivated plum. Sloes are ripe from September and they last right through the autumn. It is best to wait until after the first frosts before picking them, by which time their skins have softened and they yield more juice.

Metric	US	Imperial	
about 450g	about 1lb	about 1lb	sloes
125g	³/₄ cup	4oz	caster sugar
750ml	3¹/₃ cups	1¹/₄ pints	gin

Prick sloes with a large pin or darning needle, then put in a large, clean jar with the sugar and gin. Stir well, then cover and leave to infuse in a dark place for 3 months. Shake the jar of sloes every other day.

Before drinking, strain through muslin into a jug. You may have to do this several times, until the gin is clear. Don't squeeze the muslin or the gin will be cloudy. Pour into a clean bottle and cover.

Fruits in alcohol: Spiced Fruit and Walnut Compote in Calvados, Damsons in Mulled Wine, Tangerines in Cointreau, Apricots in Amaretto, and Black Cherries in Kirsch. (*NTPL/Andreas von Einsiedel*)

Sloe Gin Cocktails Sloe gin is usually drunk neat, but can be turned into a cocktail. Half-fill a glass with crushed ice, add a wine glass of sloe gin and a dash of orange bitters. To make Sloe Gin Fizz take one measure of sloe gin, a teaspoon of lemon juice and add soda water to taste.

Damson or plum gin Use damsons or plums instead of sloes

Sloe, Damson or Plum Vodka Use vodka instead of gin.

Victorian Cherry and Raspberry Ratafia

Fruit ratafias, or fruit liqueurs, were introduced into Britain in the seventeenth century, when brandy was considerably cheaper than it is now. A recipe of 1765 in the Yorke family papers at Erddig called for 'a Quart of the Best Brandy' and 'a Hundred Apricot Kernalls'. Many ratafias are very easy to make at home and the brandy does not have to be the best quality.

Metric	US	Imperial	
675g	1½lb	1½lb	black cherries
225g	8oz	8oz	raspberries
225g	1 cup	8oz	caster sugar
750ml	3⅓ cups	1¼ pints	brandy
1	1	1	large sprig of fresh coriander
1	1	1	cinnamon stick

Remove sufficient stones from the cherries to give 40g/¼ cup/1½oz and reserve them in a covered container in the refrigerator. Put all the cherries into a bowl and carefully mash with a potato masher, then tip into a large clean jar with the raspberries. Cover with the lid and leave for 3 days, stirring 2 or 3 times daily.

On the fourth day, crack open the reserved cherry stones with nutcrackers and remove the kernels, blanch them by pouring over boiling water and leave them to stand for 1 minute, then drain and skin them. Add the sugar to the fruit and stir until completely dissolved. Stir in the kernels with the brandy, coriander and cinnamon. Cover again and leave in a cool, dark, airy cupboard to infuse for 1 month.

To bottle, pour the infused brandy through a muslin-lined nylon sieve, discarding the coriander and cinnamon. Squeeze the fruit pulp in the muslin until every drop of liqueur is extracted, then discard. Pour the ratafia into a clean bottle, seal tightly and store in a cool place for another 3 months before drinking.

Home-made confectionery: Turkish Delight, Coconut Ice, Rum Truffles and Vanilla Fudge. (*NTPL/Andreas von Einsiedel*)

Apricot or Peach Brandy Substitute apricots or peaches for the cherries and omit the raspberries. Cut the fruit into small pieces and include a few of the fruit kernels. Continue as above.

Raspberry Brandy (Framboise) Substitute raspberries for the cherries and omit the original raspberries, as well as the spices. Continue as above.

Elderberry Liqueur

Pick the elderberries in late September when they are a deep, almost black, purple to make this rich British liqueur.

Metric	US	Imperial	
900g	2lb	2lb	elderberries
600ml	2½ cups	1 pint	brandy
350g	1¾ cups	12oz	sugar
5ml	1tsp	1tsp	ground allspice
½	½	½	cinnamon stick
1	1	1	whole clove
			large pinch of ground mace

Wash the elderberries and discard any leaves. Using a fork strip them off the stalks into a bowl. Lightly mash the fruit and stir in the other ingredients. Ladle the mixture into large jars. Cover the jars and leave in a warm place for about 4 weeks.

Strain the liqueur through fine muslin or a cotton cloth, then pour it into clean bottles. Cover and store in a cool place.

Lemon Brandy

This recipe from the Erddig archives was provided by a Mrs Harvey. Drink this as a liqueur or use as a flavouring for custards, puddings, cakes and sauces. Lemon Brandy was the 'secret' ingredient in the original Bakewell pudding and was a common flavouring in the eighteenth and nineteenth centuries. Whisky can be used instead of brandy.

Metric	US	Imperial	
3	3	3	large lemons, preferably unwaxed/organic
600ml	2½ cups	1 pint	brandy
125g	½ cup	4oz	caster sugar

Scrub and dry the lemons. Using a potato peeler remove the rind without removing any pith. Put the peel in a clean jar. Squeeze the juice from the fruit and add it to the jar with the brandy and sugar. Seal the jar and shake well to help dissolve the sugar. Store in a cool, dark place for 1-2 weeks, shaking the jar occasionally. Strain the brandy through muslin or fine cotton and pour it into bottles. It is now ready to drink.

VARIATION

Orange Brandy Use oranges instead of lemons.

Angelica Ratafia

This is made with fresh angelica, which is a lovely plant to grow in the garden. In the sixteenth century it was known as the 'herb of the angels'. Pick the stalks in the spring when they are young and tender. Drink as a delicious liqueur, or use to flavour biscuits, cakes and puddings.

Metric	US	Imperial	
225g	8oz	8oz	angelica stalks
600ml	2½ cups	1 pint	brandy
225g	1 cup	8oz	caster sugar
60ml	¼ cup	4tbsp	water

Wash and dry the angelica stalks, then cut them into small pieces and place in a large, clean jar. Cover with the brandy, then put on a lid and store in a cool, dark cupboard for 2-3 months. When you are ready to strain the brandy, stir the caster sugar and water in a pan over a moderate heat until the sugar has dissolved, then boil for 1 minute. Leave until cold.

Strain the brandy through muslin into a large jug, followed by the sugar syrup. Stir well, then pour into a clean bottle. Seal tightly and store in a cool, dry, airy cupboard.

Hawthorn Flower Liqueur

Hawthorn flowers appear in May and should be gathered on a dry day. Only the petals are used for this recipe. The liqueur has a delicate almond flavour, which makes a pleasing drink or it can be used to flavour puddings, cakes or biscuits.

Metric	US	Imperial	
125g	4oz	4oz	hawthorn flower petals
750ml	3⅓ cups	1¼ pints	brandy
175g	¾ cup	6oz	caster sugar
60ml	¼ cup	4tbsp	water

Ensure that the flowers are insect-free, then place them in a large, clean jar. Follow the instructions for Angelica Ratafia (see page 131).

Elderflower Champagne

A wonderfully refreshing summer drink, which is very easily made. Pick the elderflower blossom on a dry day when the flowers are just open – their perfume is marvellous.

Metric	US	Imperial	
4 litres	6 quarts	1 gallon	cold water
575g	2½ cups	1¼	caster sugar
30ml	2 tbsp	2 tbsp	white wine vinegar
			thinly pared rind and juice of 1 large lemon, preferably unwaxed/organic
4-6	4-6	4-6	large elderflower heads

Put the sugar into a large bowl with the water and stir until the sugar has dissolved. Stir in the vinegar, lemon rind and juice. Ensuring they are insect-free, snip the elderflowers from their stems and add to the bowl. Cover and leave to stand for 24 hours in a cool place, stirring occasionally. Strain through scalded muslin into clean screwtop bottles, squeezing the flowers to extract all the flavour. (Plastic, mineral or tonic water bottles are ideal as they are less likely to explode should the drink become too effervescent.)

Leave the champagne to stand for 2-3 weeks in a cool place, or longer, by which time it will be really bubbly and ready to drink. Drink quickly once the champagne is ready as its flavour will deteriorate.

Elderflower Cordial

Now one of the most popular bases for soft drinks, this cordial is easy to make and tastes far better than shop-bought. Use it to flavour ice-creams, fools and fruit salads.

Metric	US	Imperial	
1kg	4½ cups	2¼lb	sugar
900ml	4 cups	1½ pints	boiling water
40g	¼ cup	1½oz	citric acid
			about 15 large elderflower heads
2	2	2	lemons, sliced

Put the sugar into a large bowl with the boiling water. Stir until the sugar has dissolved, then stir in the citric acid. Ensuring they are insect-free, snip the individual flowers from their stems and add to the bowl with the sliced lemons. Cover the bowl with a clean cloth and leave to stand for 5 days, stirring daily.

Strain through scalded muslin into sterilised bottles, seal and store in the refrigerator. (The cordial will keep for up to a year in the refrigerator.) Dilute 1 part cordial with 2–3 parts soda, tonic or mineral water, add ice and serve.

Imperial Pop

This excellent recipe for ginger beer dates back to the early nineteenth century. A number of the National Trust restaurants make their own using a similar recipe.

Metric	US	Imperial	
1	1	1	lemon
450g	2¼ cups	1 lb	caster sugar
25g	3 tbsp	1 oz	cream of tartar
25g	1 oz	1 oz	fresh root ginger
4·8 litres	7 quarts	1 gallon	boiling water
25g	1 oz	1 oz	fresh yeast or 1 sachet of dried yeast

Use a potato peel to pare the rind from the lemon, avoiding the pith. Squeeze out the juice. Put into a large china bowl with the sugar and cream of tartar. Using a steak hammer or rolling pin, severely bruise the ginger without peeling it and add to the bowl. Pour over the boiling water and stir well.

When the water is just tepid, stir in the yeast. Cover and leave at least overnight to ferment. Skim and pour through a nylon sieve into screw-topped sterilised bottles. Leave for at least 2–3 days before drinking, checking after 36 hours to make sure that the ginger beer is not too fizzy. If it is in danger of exploding out of the bottles, loosen the caps very slightly.

Fresh Lemonade

Lemonade was a French invention, but English drinkers liked to add an equal quantity of white wine to make it something rather more heady! Many of the National Trust restaurants make their own versions of this wonderfully refreshing drink. This is a quick and easy recipe which is less sweet than most shop-bought lemonades, and also free from artificial colours and flavours.

Metric	US	Imperial	
3	3	3	large lemons, preferably unwaxed/organic
50-75g	¼-⅓ cup	2-3oz	sugar
about 900ml	about 4 cups	about 1½ pints	boiling water

Scrub the lemons, then slice up roughly and purée them coarsely in a food processor or blender, adding about 2 cups of the water and about a third of the sugar. Strain through a nylon sieve, then repeat the process twice more using the pulp remaining in the sieve. Add extra water and sugar to taste. Chill well, then serve decorated with mint, borage flowers and lemon slices.

Lemon Barley Water

Barley water was originally drunk as a medicine. A recipe dating to 1685 from Erddig is described as 'A Dainty Cooling Drink for a Hot Fever'. Later it became the drink of genteel Victorian ladies and is forever linked with tennis and croquet parties.

Metric	US	Imperial	
125g	¾ cup	4oz	pearl barley
50g	¼ cup	2oz	sugar cubes
4	4	4	large lemons, preferably unwaxed/organic
1·2 litres	5 cups	2 pints	boiling water

Rinse the pearl barley in a sieve under cold running water and drain well. Place in a pan and pour in cold water to cover, then bring to the boil. Reduce the heat and cook gently for 5 minutes. Pour into a sieve and rinse again, then put in a large jug or bowl. Rub each sugar cube over the rinds of the lemons to extract their oils, then add the cubes to the barley. Pour in the boiling water and stir until the sugar has dissolved. Cover with a clean cloth and leave to infuse for 3 hours or until cold.

Squeeze the juice from the lemons, add it to the barley water and strain through a nylon sieve. Cover and chill for at least 1 hour before serving with plenty of ice and lemon slices.

VARIATION

Lime Barley Water Substitute 6-8 limes (depending on size) for the lemons.

St Clement's Cordial

This lovely recipe was given to me by a Cornish friend who frequently wins prizes in local shows.

Metric	US	Imperial	
4	4	4	large juicy oranges, preferably unwaxed/organic
2	2	2	lemons, preferably unwaxed/organic
900g	4¼ cups	2lb	sugar
1·2 litres	5 cups	2 pints	boiling water
25g	3tbsp	1oz	citric acid
15g	4tsp	½oz	tartaric acid

Mince or process the fruit coarsely and place in a large bowl. Add the sugar and the boiling water and stir well. Cover and leave to steep for 24 hours. Stir in the citric and tartaric acids. Strain at least 3 times through a nylon sieve, then pour into sterilised bottles. Cover tightly and store in the refrigerator. Dilute to taste and serve chilled with orange slices, lemon balm and borage flowers.

Raspberry Shrub

This excellent summer drink tastes equally good served hot in winter. Dilute it with boiling water and sip it as the Victorians did, to soothe sore throats and to ward off colds. It also makes a good sauce for sponge puddings, ice-creams or rice puddings, or it can be used in sweet and sour dishes.

Metric	US	Imperial	
350g	1¾ cups	12oz	sugar
600ml	2½ cups	1 pint	Raspberry Vinegar (see page 45)

Heat the sugar and vinegar together gently until the sugar has completely dissolved. Bring to the boil then boil for 10 minutes. Pour into sterilised bottles, cover and leave to cool. Keep in the refrigerator for up to 6 weeks.

Dilute to taste with still or sparkling water, or soda water. For a more sophisticated drink, top up 5ml/1tsp/1tsp shrub with sparkling white wine. To make milkshakes, whisk 15ml/1tbsp/1tbsp into a glass of chilled milk.

VARIATION

Strawberry, Redcurrant, Loganberry or Blackberry Shrub Substitute the appropriate fruit vinegar for raspberry.

CHAPTER 12

Confectionery

Man discovered his fondness for sweet foods thousands of years ago, with honey and dried fruits providing the sweeteners. When sugar was first brought to Britain by the Crusaders in the late twelfth century, it was highly valued not only for cooking, but also as a medicine. Little twisted sticks of sugar resembling our modern barley-sugar sticks were a favourite form in which to take sugar against the common cold and consumption. At first, sugar was so costly it was reserved for the nobility and gentry: black teeth were a sign of wealth. Even in Elizabethan times many common folk had hardly tasted sugar, and certainly hadn't tasted the first confectionery imported from Spain and Portugal – candied citrus fruits and quince pastes (see page 96). Sweet wine was served at the final course of a feast in the Middle Ages, together with home-produced sugared spices or comfits. In Tudor and Stuart times this course expanded into the full glory of the banquet, with its marzipan or 'marchpane', crystallised and candied fruits, comfits and fondant sweets.

The banquet course went out of fashion in the early eighteenth century to be replaced by a dessert course where a great variety of sweets was served alongside jellies, syllabubs and creams. In Victorian Britain fresh fruit became the centre of the dessert course, 'bon-bons' like sugared almonds and marzipan were also offered, as they still are today with after-dinner coffee.

When chocolate arrived from Central America in the 1650s, it was enjoyed only as a drink and as a flavouring for confectionery, such as chocolate-coated almonds and fruit candies. It was not until the early nineteenth century that chocolate factories started manufacturing 'eating chocolate' in the form of chocolate bars. Fifty years later a Swiss, M. Peter, produced successful milk chocolate by mixing condensed milk with dark bitter chocolate.

Sweet-making is fun and immensely satisfying, and with a little practice very professional results can be obtained. Uncooked sweets like peppermint creams and marzipan are perfect for beginners and children. Cooked sweets require more care, but by following the recipes carefully, tasting frequently and being accurate with temperatures, success can be guaranteed. Home-made sweets and chocolates make the best of presents for people of all ages and they are often the most sought-after items on the stalls at fund-raising events.

To Make Sweets

Equipment needed

1 A large heavy-based saucepan is essential to prevent burning or sticking. Stainless steel, copper, brass or thick aluminium are the best. Enamel and non-stick pans will not stand up to high sugar boiling temperatures.

2 For guaranteed results, a sugar thermometer is recommended. To prepare a thermometer for use, it should be seasoned by placing it in a pan of cold water, allowing the water to come to the boil and then leaving it in the water to cool.

   The thermometer should be placed in the syrup with the mixture covering the bulb. It should be clipped over the side of the pan and allowed to stand upright; the reading should be taken at eye level.

3 The most useful tins for sweet-making are square or rectangular straight-sided tins. Non-stick are best as they do not need such thorough greasing.

Choosing ingredients

1 *Sugar*: Granulated sugar is suitable for many recipes as it dissolves easily. Preserving or lump sugar is used when a clear syrup without scum is required; it is also less likely to burn. Caster sugar gives a finer texture and is suitable for recipes where it is necessary to dissolve the sugar quickly. Icing sugar is the finest of white sugars and should be used when a very fine texture is required, for example for peppermint creams and marzipans. Rich soft brown sugar gives toffee a good dark colour and a rich flavour. Light brown sugar can be used for fudge.

2 *Butter*: On the whole, unsalted butter gives the best results.

3 *Glucose*: This is often added to sweets as it helps to prevent crystallisation. It can be bought in powdered or liquid form from chemists.

4 *Flavourings*: Natural flavourings are available in the form of extracts and essences. Extracts can be bought from good chemists and have a stronger and better flavour than essences. Add a very few drops at a time and taste the mixture for flavour as you go.

5 *Colourings*: Pure vegetable colourings are available from good grocers and specialist suppliers.

6 *Chocolate*: Good quality chocolate should always be used, preferably with 70% cocoa solids for plain chocolate and 40% for milk chocolate.

   To melt chocolate, break it into small pieces and place in a bowl over a pan of cold water. Make sure that the base of the bowl does not touch the water and that it is wedged into the pan so that no steam escapes around the sides of the bowl. (Humidity spoils the texture and gloss of finished chocolates and dipping is best done on a warm, dry day when there is no other steamy cooking taking place.) Heat the water gently, but don't allow it to boil. Remove from the heat and stir the chocolate until it is completely melted. If it starts to harden again before you have finished dipping, simply reheat it gently in the same way.

Sugar Boiling

Making sure the sugar reaches the correct temperature is the secret of successful sweet making. Here are some guidelines:

1 Dissolve the sugar in the water very slowly. Don't allow it to boil until completely dissolved.
2 Once the sugar is boiling, remove any crystals that form on the sides of the pan with a clean brush dipped in hot water. Resist the temptation to stir the sugar unless the recipe actually tells you to do so.

Sugar Boiling Temperatures

1 *Soft ball*: 112–116°C/235–240°F
This is used for fudges. To test without a thermometer, place a small drop of the syrup into cold water. If rolled with the fingers the syrup should form a soft ball. If not, the syrup should be boiled a bit longer.
2 *Hard ball*: 120–130°C/250–265°F
This is used for caramels. To test without a thermometer, drop a small amount of the syrup into cold water and the small ball which forms should be hard enough to hold its shape.
3 *Soft crack*: 132–143°C/270–290°F
This is used for toffee. When dropped into cold water, the syrup separates into threads which become hard, but not brittle.

Vanilla Fudge

Home-made fudge is a year-round favourite with everyone. Make several batches with different flavourings to provide an interesting assortment in a gift box. Use this basic recipe and substitute other flavourings for the vanilla – white or plain chocolate, stem ginger, glacé cherries, coconut or nuts – or use muscovado sugar for the granulated and cream for the milk.

Metric	US	Imperial	
450g	1lb	1lb	granulated sugar
400g	1¹/₃ cups	14oz	tin of condensed milk
50g	4tbsp	2oz	butter
30ml	2tbsp	2tbsp	milk
150ml	²/₃ cup	¹/₄ pint	water
5ml	1tsp	1tsp	natural vanilla extract

Butter a 23cm/9in square tin.

Place the sugar, condensed milk, butter, milk and water into a heavy-based pan. Heat gently together until the sugar has completely dissolved, then bring slowly to a fierce boil. Reduce the heat by about one-third, to a rolling boil. Cook for 8-10 minutes, stirring constantly until a little dropped into a cup of cold water forms a soft ball when rolled between finger and thumb. If you are using a sugar thermometer, boil to 'soft ball' stage 112-116°C/235-240°F. Remove from the heat, add the vanilla and beat with an electric beater for 2-3 minutes until thick.

Pour into the prepared tin and leave to cool. When almost set, mark into squares and leave to cool completely. When cold, cut up the fudge and remove from the tin. Store in an airtight container for up to 2 weeks.

Coconut Ice

The advent of desiccated coconut (the dried shredded flesh of the nut) in Victorian times led to its widespread use in cookery. This popular sweet makes a very attractive present at Christmas. Unfortunately it goes stale quickly, so make it no more than a few days before you intend giving it.

Metric	US	Imperial	
450g	2¼ cups	1 lb	caster sugar
150ml	⅔ cup	¼ pint	milk or single cream
150g	5oz	5oz	desiccated coconut
			cochineal or pink food colouring

Lightly oil a shallow 20 × 15cm/8 × 6in tin with a tasteless vegetable oil and set aside.

Place the sugar and milk in a heavy pan over low heat and stir until the sugar dissolves. Increase the heat and bring to the boil, then allow the mixture to boil gently for about 10 minutes or until a little dropped into cold water forms a soft ball between finger and thumb (112-116°C/235-240°F on a sugar thermometer).

Remove from the heat and beat in the coconut. Quickly pour half the mixture into the oiled tin and spread it evenly, using a wet knife. Stir a few drops of colouring into the remaining mixture so that it turns pale pink. Spread this evenly over the white coconut mixture and leave to cool. As soon as it begins to set, mark the mixture out into neat squares.

Leave until completely cold and set firm. Cut or break the coconut ice into pieces and eat it within a few days, as it is best enjoyed slightly moist.

Chocolate Marzipan Slices

Marzipan was first used to make the 'subtleties' or moulded paste figures of allegorical animals and castles which were placed before an admiring audience at the end of each course of a great medieval feast. By Elizabeth I's reign, a 'marchpane', or flat cake of decorated and gilded marzipan frosted with sugar and rose-water provided the centrepiece at the banquet course. In Georgian times this was united with plum cake and covered with thick icing, hence our modern wedding and Christmas cakes.

Metric	US	Imperial	
225g	8oz	8oz	almond paste, preferably home-made
15ml	1 tbsp	1 tbsp	cocoa powder
			a few drops of pink or lilac colouring
15ml	1 tbsp	1 tbsp	apricot jam, preferably home-made
75g	3oz	3oz	good-quality plain chocolate

Divide the almond paste into 3 equal-sized pieces. Knead the cocoa powder into one piece, the food colouring into another and leave the third piece plain. Roll each piece of almond paste into a strip measuring $19 \times 2 \cdot 5$ cm/$7^{1}/_{2} \times 1$ in and about $1 \cdot 25$ cm/$^{1}/_{2}$ in thick. Press the jam through a sieve. Brush the piece of cocoa paste with a little of the jam and position the pastel-coloured paste on top. Brush this with a little jam and position the plain paste over this. Trim the sides of the paste to form a neat block.

Melt the chocolate in a bowl over a pan of simmering water. Spoon a little of the melted chocolate along the cocoa-flavoured side of the paste and chill for 5 minutes until set. Lay the paste on a piece of greaseproof paper with the chocolate-coated side on the bottom. Spread the remaining melted chocolate over the top and sides of the paste until completely covered. Leave in a cool place until set.

Dip a large knife into very hot water and quickly dry it, then use to cut the chocolate-coated marzipan into slices. Dip and wipe the knife occasionally to keep it hot and clean.

French Nougat

The name of this chewy confection comes from the Latin *nux* which means nut. Glacé fruits are an addition to the original nougat. Experiment by adding different fruits and nuts.

Metric	US	Imperial	
450g	2$^{1}/_{4}$ cups	1 lb	granulated sugar
225g	8oz	8oz	powdered glucose
150ml	$^{2}/_{3}$ cup	$^{1}/_{4}$ pint	water
2	2	2	egg whites
125g	1 cup	4oz	blanched almonds, toasted and chopped
50g	2oz	2oz	glacé cherries, chopped
25g	1oz	1oz	angelica, chopped

Dampen the inside of an 20×15 cm/8×6 inch shallow tin and line it with edible rice paper.

Put the sugar, glucose and water in a heavy-based pan and heat gently until the sugar and glucose have completely dissolved. Bring to the boil, then simmer gently until a little of the syrup mixture dropped into cold water forms a hard ball between finger and thumb. (If using a sugar thermometer, it should read 132-143°C/270-290°F or soft crack stage.)

Beat the egg whites until stiff, then gradually beat in the syrup. As soon as the mixture begins to thicken, add the nuts, cherries and angelica. Mix well, then pour into the prepared tin. Cover with more rice paper, then a sheet of non-stick baking parchment. Press down with a similar tin on top containing heavy weights. Leave in a cool place for at least 12 hours until set. Cut into bars, then wrap in greaseproof or waxed paper and store in an airtight tin for up to 2 weeks.

Panforte

This Tuscan speciality has been eaten since the Middle Ages, when spices were first imported. Traditionally made for Christmas, it is exceedingly rich and should be served in small slices. This particular recipe is based on one by Antonio Carluccio, but the candied pumpkin, which is not very easy to find, has been replaced by candied orange and lemon peel, candied apricots and candied pineapple. The flavour may not be authentic, but it is very good. If you can find candied pumpkin, use 250g/9oz/9oz and omit the replacement ingredients.

Metric	US	Imperial	
250g	2 cups	9oz	almonds, blanched and toasted
150g	1 cup	5oz	walnuts or pecans
50g	2oz	2oz	candied citron peel
50g	2oz	2oz	candied orange peel
25g	1oz	1oz	candied lemon peel
125g	4oz	4oz	candied apricots
50g	2oz	2oz	candied pineapple
10ml	2tsp	2tsp	ground cinnamon
10ml	2tsp	2tsp	ground coriander
2·5ml	½tsp	½tsp	freshly grated nutmeg
200g	1 cup	7oz	plain flour
200g	1 cup	7oz	icing sugar
200g	1 cup	7oz	clear honey
15ml	1tbsp	1tbsp	water
			icing sugar to finish

Line 20cm/8in round cake tin, (about 4cm/1½in deep) with edible rice paper. Pre-heat the oven to 160°C/325°F/gas mark 3.

Mix the almonds and walnuts or pecans together in a bowl. Cut the candied peel into small strips and the apricots and pineapple into small chunks, then add to the bowl with the spices. Add the flour and mix in very well. Put the icing sugar, honey and water into a heavy-based pan. Heat gently until dissolved, then increase the heat so that the mixture bubbles. Stir with a wooden spoon until it forms a dense, pale-brown caramel. Pour on to the fruit and nut mixture and mix until smooth.

Spread the mixture in the prepared tin, levelling the top with a spatula. Bake for about 30 minutes, then remove and leave to cool in the tin. Turn out and dredge with icing sugar to finish. Wrap in waxed paper and store in an airtight container. Panforte keeps well for several months, so it makes the ideal gift.

Tiffin

This is a classy version of an old childhood favourite. It is exceedingly rich and is best served with after-dinner coffee. Give as a present that brings back memories to the older generation or introduce youngsters to a new experience. Use almonds or Brazil nuts instead, or a mixture of nuts.

Metric	US	Imperial	
50g	¼ cup	2oz	seedless raisins
30ml	2 tbsp	2 tbsp	brandy or orange juice
175g	6oz	6oz	good-quality plain chocolate
125g	1 stick	4oz	unsalted butter
			pinch of salt
125g	4oz	4oz	whole candied peel
150g	¾ cup	5oz	digestive biscuits, broken into small pieces
75g	3oz	3oz	hazelnuts, toasted and roughly chopped

Line a 15–20cm/7–8in square shallow baking tin with edible rice paper.

Soak the raisins in the brandy or orange juice for 30–60 minutes. Break the chocolate up roughly and place in a bowl set over a pan of simmering water with the butter and salt. As soon as the chocolate has melted, turn off the heat. Stir in the raisins and all the remaining ingredients. Turn the mixture into the prepared tin and press down evenly. Chill in the refrigerator for several hours or overnight until firm. Turn the tiffin out of the tin and break it into pieces or cut into 16 squares. Store in an airtight container.

Bonfire Toffee

This is known as 'Plot Toffee' in Yorkshire, where it is traditionally enjoyed on Bonfire Night, 5 November.

Metric	US	Imperial	
125g	1 stick	4oz	butter
225g	1 cup	8oz	black treacle
225g	1 cup	8oz	demerara sugar

Butter a 20cm/8in shallow square tin.

Melt the butter in a large heavy-based pan, then add the treacle and sugar. Heat gently, stirring until the sugar has dissolved, then stop stirring and bring back to the boil. Lower the heat and simmer gently for about 30 minutes to soft crack stage, 132-143°C/270-290°F. If you do not have a thermometer, test by dropping a little of the mixture into cold water – it should separate into threads when pulled and become hard, but not brittle. Don't stir the mixture after the sugar has dissolved otherwise the toffee will crystallise.

Pour the toffee into the prepared tin, cool for about 5 minutes, then mark it into squares and leave to set. Break into pieces when cold and wrap in waxed or grease-proof paper. Store in an airtight tin.

Chocolate Rum Truffles

Traditionally eaten at Christmas, these delectable 'melt in the mouth' morsels first appeared in the Army and Navy Stores catalogue of 1926. Make sure your hands are very cold before you shape these truffles.

Metric	US	Imperial	
175g	6oz	6oz	good-quality plain or milk chocolate
125ml	1/4 cup	4floz	double cream
30ml	2tbsp	2tbsp	rum or Cointreau
			cocoa powder or icing sugar to finish

Break the chocolate into small pieces. Bring the cream just to the boil in a heavy-based pan. Remove from the heat and stir in the chocolate until melted. Add the liqueur and leave the mixture in the fridge until very firm.

Dust your hands with cocoa powder or icing sugar, then take a small teaspoon of the mixture in the palm of your hands and roll into a ball about 2cm/³⁄₄in in diameter. Sieve a little cocoa powder or icing sugar on to a plate and drop the truffle into it, gently rolling it around until completely covered. Repeat until the mixture is used up. (You will make about 30 balls each about 2cm/³⁄₄in in diameter.) Leave the truffles in a cool place, covered, to harden a little before eating. They may be stored for up to 1 week in the refrigerator.

Hazelnut Truffles

Truffles can be coated with chocolate instead of being rolled in cocoa powder or icing sugar. Use other nuts for a change.

Metric	US	Imperial	
70g	²/₃ cup	2½ oz	hazelnuts
125ml	¼ cup	4 fl oz	double cream
175g	6oz	6oz	good-quality plain or milk chocolate, broken into pieces
30ml	2 tbsp	2 tbsp	brandy or Cointreau
			For the decoration
200g	7oz	7oz	good quality plain chocolate
25g	1oz	1oz	good quality milk chocolate

Reserve 30 whole hazelnuts and lightly toast the remainder. Finely chop the toasted hazelnuts.

Bring the cream just to the boil in a heavy-based pan. Remove from the heat and stir in the chocolate until melted. Turn into a small bowl, then add the liqueur and chopped hazelnuts. Chill until very firm.

Take a small teaspoonful of the mixture in the palm of your hands and roll into a ball about 2cm/³/₄in in diameter. Repeat with the remaining mixture to make about 30 small balls. Press a reserved hazelnut into the top of each and chill the truffles until firm. (You can store these uncoated truffles for up to 1 week in the fridge, if you wish, before coating.)

To coat them, place a wire rack over a sheet of greaseproof paper to catch the drips and put the truffles on the rack. Melt the plain chocolate in a bowl over a pan of gently simmering water.

Using a dessertspoon, spoon a little chocolate over a truffle until it is thinly coated. Repeat with the remaining truffles.

To finish, melt the milk chocolate, spoon into a greaseproof paper piping bag and snip off just the tip. (Alternatively, use a nylon bag fitted with a writing nozzle.) Pipe swirls of chocolate onto the tops of the truffles, then leave to set. Keep in a cool place before eating.

A selection of home-made biscuits, sweet and savoury.
(*NTPL/Andreas von Einsiedel*)

Rose Turkish Delight

This Turkish sweetmeat is called *rahat lokoum* (literally 'throat's ease') in its home country and was originally known in English as 'lumps of delight'. Its present name was first recorded in 1877.

Metric	US	Imperial	
30ml	2 tbsp	2 tbsp	rose-water
25g	4 packages	1oz	gelatine
270ml	1 cup	9 fl oz	cold water
450g	2¼ cups	1lb	sugar
			few drops of pink food colouring
25g	¼ cup	1oz	icing sugar
25g	¼ cup	1oz	cornflour

Mix 15ml/1tbsp/1tbsp of the rose-water with 45ml/3tbsps/3tbsps of cold water in a small basin. Sprinkle the gelatine evenly over the liquid, but don't stir it in. Leave to stand for about 5 minutes or until the gelatine has absorbed the liquid and swollen into a spongy mass.

Gently heat the sugar in the 270ml/1 cup/9 fl oz water in a heavy-based pan, stirring until the sugar has completely dissolved. Add the gelatine mixture to the pan stirring constantly until it has completely melted, then bring to the boil. Boil over a medium heat for 20 minutes, then remove from the heat and add the remaining rose-water and the colouring. Pour into a wetted 20 × 15cm/8 × 6in tin and chill for 24 hours until set.

Sieve the icing sugar and cornflour together and sprinkle evenly over a piece of greaseproof paper. Turn the Turkish delight out onto this paper and cut it into 2·5cm/1in squares with a sharp knife. Toss well in the sugar mixture, then pack in an airtight container lined with waxed paper. Mix more icing sugar and cornflour together in equal quantities, then sprinkle liberally over the sweets, to stop them sticking together before covering the container.

The nineteenth-century still-room at Tatton Park, with biscuits and cucumber sandwiches. (*NTPL/Andreas von Einsiedel*)

Peppermint Creams

Uncooked peppermint creams are extremely simple to make but very effective. They can be finished by dipping half of the sweet into plain chocolate. If you use oil of peppermint, remember that it is much stronger than essence, so use it sparingly.

Metric	US	Imperial	
450g	4 cups	1 lb	icing sugar
5 ml	1 tsp	1 tsp	lemon juice
1	1	1	egg white, lightly whisked
			a few drops of oil of peppermint, or peppermint essence
			green food colouring (optional)

Sieve the icing sugar into a bowl and mix with the lemon juice and enough egg white to make a pliable mixture. Flavour with peppermint and tint a very pale green if you wish. (The sweets look attractive if you colour just half the mixture and then pack up some white and some green sweets together.)

Knead on a work surface lightly dusted with icing sugar, then roll out 6mm/¼ in thick. Cut into small rounds with a 2·5cm/1in plain pastry cutter or form into balls and flatten slightly with a rolling pin. Leave in a cool place for 24 hours to set and dry.

Chocolate Gingers

These are for real ginger lovers. If a milder flavour is preferred, replace half the crystallised ginger with raisins.

Metric	US	Imperial	
175g	6oz	6oz	good-quality white chocolate
50g	2oz	2oz	crystallised ginger, chopped
100g	¾ cup	3½ oz	blanched almonds, lightly toasted and chopped
175g	6oz	6oz	good-quality plain chocolate

Line a baking tray with greaseproof paper.

Break the white chocolate into pieces, then melt it in a bowl over a pan of simmering water. Stir in the crystallised ginger and almonds, then place teaspoonfuls of the mixture on the prepared baking tray. Chill until firm.

Break the plain chocolate into pieces, then melt in a bowl over a pan of simmering water. Using a thin skewer or cocktail stick, dip each chocolate into the plain melted chocolate allowing any excess to drip back into the bowl. Place on a clean sheet of greaseproof paper to set.

CHAPTER 13

Biscuits and Cookies

The first true biscuits were ship's biscuits; literally, rusks of twice-cooked bread, hence the name, from the Latin *panis biscoctus*. Bakers put them into their beehive ovens to dry out after the loaves of bread had been removed. In Tudor England, richer biscuits, often referred to as 'cakes', were made to eat with spiced wine and mead after dinner. However, they were still dried out in the oven after their initial baking, so tended to be hard. This practice was abandoned in the eighteenth century when a wide range of biscuits was developed to accompany jellies and creamy puddings for dessert and to eat at the tea-table. The range has been growing ever since; just take a look at today's groaning supermarket shelves.

Cookies, on the other hand, have come to us from America. Defining the difference between a cookie and a biscuit is almost impossible. On some occasions a cookie is softer and more cake-like and on others it is barely distinguishable from a biscuit. What matters is that they taste equally delicious and make acceptable gifts.

Although the majority of biscuits and cookies are simple to make and much cheaper than shop-bought, very few people bother these days. And yet everyone loves home-made biscuits, as the National Trust restaurants and tea-rooms can testify. They all serve home-made shortbread and a variety of biscuits with morning coffee and afternoon tea, and have trouble keeping up with demand.

Remember to pack your biscuits in airtight containers to give as gifts so that they remain as crisp as when first baked.

Amaretti Macaroons

First made in France, they became very fashionable in Georgian times in England; today they are made in various sizes in Italy. Make small ones for petit fours and larger ones for tea, or to accompany ice-creams and other creamy desserts.

Metric	US	Imperial	
125g	1 cup	4oz	ground almonds
15g	1/2 oz	1/2 oz	ground rice
225g	1 cup	8oz	caster sugar
1·25ml	1/4 tsp	1/4 tsp	ratafia essence
2	2	2	egg whites
12	12	12	blanched almonds, halved
1	1	1	egg white, beaten, for glazing

Line a baking tray with edible rice paper.
Pre-heat the oven to 180°C/350°F/gas mark 4.

Mix together the ground almonds, ground rice and sugar in a bowl. Add the ratafia essence to the unbeaten egg whites and mix into the dry ingredients. Cream to a smooth paste in a blender, then put the mixture into a piping bag with a plain 1cm/½in nozzle.

Rule the rice paper into 5cm/2in squares, then pipe the mixture into the centre of each square, making the biscuits about 2·5cm/1in in diameter. Flatten slightly and press an almond half into the centre of each macaroon. Brush lightly with the beaten white of an egg.

Bake for about 20 minutes, or until golden brown. Remove from the oven and cool on a wire rack. Cut off the rice paper around each macaroon. Store in an airtight container for 1-2 weeks, although as macaroons tend to harden with time, it is better to eat them while still fresh.

Brandy Snaps

These scrumptious biscuits have ancient origins; they were made on a flat wafering iron over the open fire in Elizabethan England. As soon as they were cooked to a golden brown they were lifted from the hot iron plate and rolled around a small wooden stick to set in the curled shape that we still appreciate today. Serve for tea (filled with cream if you wish) or with creamy desserts. Tiny brandy snaps are wonderful at the end of dinner with coffee.

Metric	US	Imperial	
125g	8 tbsp	4oz	butter
125g	½ cup	4oz	demerara sugar
125g	½ cup	4oz	golden syrup
125g	1 cup	4oz	plain flour
			pinch of salt
5ml	1 tsp	1 tsp	ground ginger
5ml	1 tsp	1 tsp	lemon juice
2-3	2-3	2-3	drops natural vanilla extract

Well grease 2 baking trays.
Pre-heat the oven to 160°C/325°F/gas mark 3.

Put the butter, sugar and syrup into a heavy-based pan. Heat gently, stirring until the butter has melted and the sugar has completely dissolved. Leave to cool slightly. Sieve the flour with the salt and ginger into the mixture, then stir well, adding the lemon juice and vanilla extract.

Put teaspoonfuls of the mixture on to a prepared baking tray at least 10cm/4in apart. Bake for about 8 minutes until a darker brown round the edges, then remove from the oven and leave to cool for 2–3 minutes. Remove each biscuit from the tin with a palette knife, turn it over, then roll around the handle of a wooden spoon. (Put back in the oven for a few seconds if the biscuits harden too much to handle.) Leave on a wire rack to cool completely. Store in an airtight container.

VARIATIONS

Chocolate-dipped Brandy Snaps Melt 50g/2oz/2oz plain chocolate in a bowl over a pan of hot, boiling water. Dip the cold brandy snaps to half cover them.

Brandy Snap Tuiles Instead of rolling around the handle of a wooden spoon, wrap them around a wooden rolling pin.

Sticky Pecan Brownies

Everybody loves these American cookies, so they make an ideal gift, particularly at Christmas. Walnuts can be used instead of pecans if you wish.

Metric	US	Imperial	
125g	1 stick	4oz	unsalted butter
175g	³/₄ cup	6oz	caster sugar
75g	¹/₃ cup	3oz	soft dark brown sugar
125g	4oz	4oz	good quality plain chocolate
15ml	1 tbsp	1 tbsp	golden syrup
50g	1 cup	2oz	plain flour
2·5ml	¹/₂ tsp	¹/₂ tsp	baking powder
2	2	2	medium eggs
5ml	1 tsp	1 tsp	natural vanilla essence
175g	²/₃ cup	6oz	pecans, coarsely chopped

Grease and flour an 20cm/8in square deep cake tin.
Preheat the oven to 180°C/350°F/gas mark 4.

Put the butter, sugars, chocolate and syrup in a small non-stick pan and heat gently, stirring until the mixture is smooth and the chocolate has melted. Remove from the heat and leave to cool.

Sieve the flour and baking powder into the chocolate mixture. Beat the eggs and the vanilla together, then pour into the chocolate mixture. Add the chopped nuts and stir well to mix.

Pour the mixture into the prepared tin and bake for 25 minutes, or until the edges of the brownie are crisp and beginning to shrink from the sides of the tin. The inside must still be soft to the touch.

Leave to cool completely in the tin, then cut into squares: there should be enough for 9 pieces. Store in an airtight tin.

Chocolate-Dipped Almond Cookies

Serve these as petit fours with after-dinner coffee, or make a batch as a birthday surprise for a friend. They can be made well in advance and frozen undecorated for up to 3 months. Thaw on a wire rack at room temperature for 2 hours before decorating.

Metric	US	Imperial	
225g	1 cup	8oz	unsalted butter, softened
175g	³/₄ cup	6oz	caster sugar
1	1	1	large egg yolk
			few drops of natural vanilla extract
350g	2¹/₂ cups	12oz	plain flour
			pinch of salt
125g	³/₄ cup	4oz	blanched almonds, finely chopped
			For the decoration
125g	4oz	4oz	good-quality plain chocolate
125g	³/₄ cup	4oz	flaked almonds, toasted and roughly chopped

Line 2 baking trays with non-stick baking parchment.

Cream the butter with the sugar until light and fluffy, then beat in the egg yolk and vanilla extract. Stir in the flour, salt and almonds. Divide the mixture in half and roll into 2 sausage shapes about 4cm/1¹/₂in in diameter. Wrap in greaseproof paper and chill for 1 hour.

Preheat the oven to 180°C/350°F/gas mark 4.

Using a sharp knife, cut the dough into 1·25cm/¹/₂in thick slices and place on the prepared trays about 4cm/1¹/₂in apart. Bake for 15–18 minutes until lightly browned. Leave to cool a little on the trays, then transfer to a wire rack to cool completely.

To decorate the cookies, melt the chocolate in a bowl over a pan of simmering water. Place the chopped almonds in a small basin. Have a sheet of non-stick parchment ready on a baking tray. Half-dip each cookie into the chocolate, then into the almonds. Place on the paper and leave to cool until the chocolate hardens.

Chocolate Chunk Cookies

Unlike biscuits, American cookies should be crisp on the outside and soft in the middle even when cold. Children and adults alike adore these.

Metric	US	Imperial	
250g	18 tbsp	9oz	sunflower margarine
50g	¼ cup	2oz	caster sugar
125g	½ cup	4oz	soft light brown sugar
10ml	2tsp	2tsp	natural vanilla extract
1	1	1	small egg
300g	2¼ cups	11oz	plain flour
5ml	1tsp	1tsp	baking powder
75g	½ cup	3oz	walnuts, roughly chopped
250g	9oz	9oz	good-quality plain chocolate, roughly chopped

Line 2 baking trays with non-stick baking parchment.
Preheat the oven to 160°C/325°F/gas mark 3.

Beat the margarine, sugars and vanilla essence in a bowl until light and fluffy. Whisk the egg lightly with a fork, then beat 30ml/2tbsp/2tbsp into the creamed mixture. (Discard any left-over egg or the cookies will spread too much.) Sieve the flour and baking powder into the creamed mixture, then add the walnuts and chocolate. Stir well to bind.

Divide the mixture into about 24 pieces each weighing 40g/1½oz/1½oz. Roll these pieces into balls, then flatten very slightly and arrange on the prepared baking trays. Bake for about 10 minutes, or until pale golden brown; the centres should feel soft. Leave to cool on the trays for 5 minutes, then transfer to a wire rack to cool completely.

Kathleen's Cornish Fairings

London-born Kathleen came westwards to work for the Robartes family at Lanhydrock House in Cornwall as a kitchen maid and married Bill Stevens the footman. She very kindly parted with her recipe for these traditional Cornish biscuits, once sold at West Country fairs, hence their name.

Metric	US	Imperial	
30ml	2tbsp	2tbsp	golden syrup
225g	1 cup	8oz	margarine
175g	6oz	6oz	caster sugar
350g	2 cups	12oz	self-raising flour
1·25ml	¼tsp	¼tsp	bicarbonate of soda
10ml	2tsp	2tsp	ground ginger

Grease 2 baking trays.
Pre-heat the oven to 180°C/350°F/gas mark 4.

In a large pan, melt the syrup and margarine together over a low heat. Remove from the heat and stir in the sugar. Sieve the flour, bicarbonate of soda and ginger together into the pan, then stir together to form a dough. Roll into small balls, each about the size of a walnut, and place on the baking trays, leaving plenty of room between each one as they spread during cooking. Bake for about 10 minutes, or until golden brown and well spread. Leave to cool on the trays for a few minutes, then transfer to a wire rack to cool completely. Store in an airtight container.

Luxury Florentines

These moist little biscuits coated with white and plain chocolate are perfect to serve with after-dinner coffee. They make a splendid gift for any occasion – remember this recipe on birthdays, Mother's and Father's days, or as an alternative to Easter eggs.

Metric	US	Imperial	
40g	3 tbsp	1½ oz	unsalted butter
40g	1½ oz	1½ oz	golden syrup
15g	2 tbsp	½ oz	plain flour
25g	1 oz	1 oz	blanched almonds, finely chopped
25g	1 oz	1 oz	natural glacé cherries washed, dried and chopped
15g	½ oz	½ oz	stem ginger in syrup, washed, dried and chopped
40g	1½ oz	1½ oz	dried mixed fruit
40g	1½ oz	1½ oz	good-quality plain chocolate
40g	1½ oz	1½ oz	good-quality white chocolate

Line several baking sheets with non-stick baking parchment.
Preheat the oven to 180°C/350°F/gas mark 4.

Melt the butter and syrup in a heavy-based pan. Stir in all the remaining ingredients, except the chocolates and leave to stand for 2–3 minutes.

Place small teaspoonfuls of the mixture onto the baking trays in batches, spacing them well apart as the mixture spreads during cooking. Bake for 7–10 minutes until golden brown. Leave on the trays for 1 minute, then transfer to a wire rack to cool completely.

Melt the chocolates in separate bowls over pans of simmering water. Coat the flat side of half the florentines with melted plain chocolate and the remaining half with white chocolate. Use a fork to mark wavy lines in the chocolate and leave to for about 30 minutes or until set. Store in an airtight tin for up to 3 days. They soften if kept for any longer.

Julia's Rich Orange Shortbread

Crisp, buttery Scottish shortbread, which was originally made with oatmeal, dates from the twelfth century and possibly earlier. It was made in a circular shape to represent the sun with the traditional pinched edge supposed to represent the sun's rays. This recipe comes from a good friend who arrived for New Year celebrations bearing a basket of shortbread to share with us all. It was, indeed, a memorable gift.

Metric	US	Imperial	
225g	1 cup	8oz	slightly salted butter, softened
125g	1 cup	4oz	icing sugar, sieved
125g	1 cup	4oz	cornflour
225g	2 cups	8oz	plain flour
			grated rind of 1 large orange, preferably unwaxed/organic
			caster sugar for sprinkling

Lightly butter a 15 × 25cm/6 × 10in deep baking tin.

Cream the butter and icing sugar together until light and fluffy, then sieve in the flours. Add the orange rind, then mix to a dough with one hand. (Don't over handle the dough or your shortbread will be tough.) Press the dough into the prepared tin, flattening it evenly with the palm of your hand. Prick all over with a fork, then chill in the refrigerator for at least 1 hour.

Heat the oven to 160°C/325°F/gas mark 3.

Bake the shortbread for about 40 minutes until pale golden. Remove from the oven, turning it off. Mark 16 shortbread into fingers and sprinkle with sugar. Put back in the oven for 10 minutes to dry slightly in the residual heat.

Cut the shortbread into fingers as soon as it is removed from the oven. Leave in the tin until cold, then store in an airtight tin.

VARIATIONS

Traditional Butter Shortbread Omit the orange rind.

Ginger Shortbread Sieve 15ml/1tsp/1tsp ground ginger with the flour and add 25g/1oz/1oz stem or crystallised ginger finely chopped instead of the orange rind. Ice with a little glacé icing flavoured with ground ginger if you wish.

Almond Shortbread Add 50g/2oz/2oz blanched almonds, finely chopped, and 50g/2oz/2oz mixed candied peel, finely chopped (optional), instead of the grated orange rind.

Cherry Shortbread Add 50g/2oz/2oz glacé cherries, finely chopped, instead of the orange rind.

Butterscotch Shortbread

This is another excellent variation on the popular classic biscuit.

Metric	US	Imperial	
125g	1 stick	4oz	slightly salted butter, softened
50g	¼ cup	2oz	soft dark brown sugar
2·5ml	½ tsp	½ tsp	natural vanilla extract
150g	1 cup	5oz	plain flour
25g	¼ cup	1oz	ground almonds
			caster sugar for sprinkling

Lightly butter a 23cm/9in square baking tin and dust it with flour.

Cream the butter and sugar until light and fluffy. Blend in the vanilla extract, then gradually work in the sieved flour and the ground almonds until completely blended. Press the dough into the prepared tin and pat out evenly with your hands. Prick all over with a fork, then chill in the fridge for about 1 hour.

Pre-heat the oven to 160°C/325°F/gas mark 3.

Bake for 30-35 minutes or until the top feels firm when touched gently. Leave the shortbread to cool in the tin on a wire rack for about 10 minutes. Cut into squares and sprinkle with sugar.

Remove from the tin when cold, then store in an airtight container.

Chocolate Shortbread

Serve this addictive shortbread with tea or coffee, or for dessert with vanilla or nutty ice-cream. The recipe uses semolina instead of icing sugar to make the shortbread 'short'. Make sure you use best-quality milk chocolate (one with at least 30% cocoa solids – preferably 40%).

Metric	US	Imperial	
275g	1¼ cups	10oz	unsalted butter, softened
175g	¾ cup	6oz	caster sugar
175g	6oz	6oz	milk chocolate, cut into chunks
225g	2 cups	8oz	plain flour
125g	1 cup	4oz	semolina

Lightly butter a 23 × 33cm / 9 × 13in Swiss-roll tin.

Cream the butter and sugar together until light and fluffy. Mix in the chocolate chunks very carefully, then the sieved flour and semolina. Work with one hand into a dough, but don't overwork or the shortbread will be tough. Press the mixture into the prepared tin using the palms of your hands, then prick all over with a fork. Chill in the fridge for about 1 hour.

Pre-heat the oven to 160°C / 325°F / gas mark 3.

Bake in the oven for about 40-50 minutes, or until pale golden round the edges. Cut into squares or fingers while still hot, then leave to cool completely in the tin.

Almond Tuiles

These delicate French biscuits are delicious with coffee, or as an accompaniment to creamy desserts. They are known as 'tuiles' because they resemble the curved tiles on an old French farmhouse roof. The biscuits are extremely fragile, so pack them carefully in an airtight container lined with crumpled greaseproof or tissue paper if you are presenting them as a gift.

Metric	US	Imperial	
75g	6 tbsp	3oz	butter
75g	1/2 cup	3oz	caster sugar
50g	1/4 cup	2oz	plain flour
			pinch of salt
75g	1/2 cup	3oz	blanched almonds

Well grease 2 baking trays.
Pre-heat the oven to 200°C / 400°F / gas mark 6.

Soften the butter, then add the sugar and beat well until light and fluffy. Sieve the flour and salt together, then stir into the mixture with the almonds. Place small teaspoons of the mixture into the prepared baking tray leaving plenty of space between, because the biscuits will spread during cooking. Flatten the biscuits with a wet fork. Bake for 6-8 minutes until just coloured.

Allow to stand for a few seconds before removing carefully from the tin with a palette knife. Curl on to a rolling pin and leave until set into curved shapes. (If some of the biscuits have hardened before you've had time to shape them, put them back in the oven for a few seconds to soften them.) Continue baking and shaping the mixture until it is all used.

Store the biscuits in an airtight container; they also freeze well.

Cotehele's Cinnamon Shorties

The restaurant in the medieval barn at Cotehele in Cornwall serves these spicy biscuits with morning coffee.

Metric	US	Imperial	
175g	1 cup	6oz	wholemeal flour
25g	2tsp	2tsp	ground cinnamon
125g	¾ cup	4oz	butter, at room temperature
40g	1½oz	1½oz	muscovado sugar
			beaten egg white to glaze
			flaked almonds to decorate

Pre-heat the oven to 180°C/350°F/gas mark 4.
Lightly grease a baking tray.

Sieve the flour and cinnamon together into a bowl, adding the bran remaining in the sieve. Rub in the butter until the mixture resembles breadcrumbs, then stir in the sugar. Knead the mixture together with your hands to form a dough, then divide it into about 14 pieces. Roll each piece into a ball and place on the baking tray. Flatten each one with your fingers, then glaze with egg white. Sprinkle with almonds and bake for 20–25 minutes. Remove from the oven and leave to cool slightly on the tray. Transfer to a wire rack and leave until completely cold. Store in an airtight tin.

Parmesan Shortbreads

These crisp cheesy biscuits are perfect with pre-dinner drinks and a good alternative to sweet biscuits as a gift for those who have a 'savoury tooth'.

Metric	US	Imperial	
75g	½ cup	3oz	plain flour
1·25ml	¼tsp	¼tsp	salt
75g	½ cup	3oz	freshly grated Parmesan cheese
75g	6tbsp	3oz	unsalted butter, creamed until very soft
10ml	2tsp	2tsp	olive oil

Very lightly butter a baking tray.

Sieve the flour and salt together into a bowl, then mix in all the other ingredients until well combined. Work into a crumbly dough with your hand, then roll out into a sausage shape, about 23cm/9in long on a lightly floured working surface. Chill for 30 minutes in the fridge.

Pre-heat the oven to 150°C/300°F/gas mark 2.

Cut the dough into thin slices with a sharp knife and place on the prepared baking tray. Bake in the oven for 20-25 minutes, or until pale golden brown. Cool slightly on a wire rack, then serve warm with drinks, or cool completely and store in an airtight tin .

Cheese Straws

This is the best recipe for cheese straws that I have come across. If you don't like the taste of Parmesan – or the smell of it cooking – use a good-flavoured Cheddar. The cut straws can be frozen uncooked, then baked straight from the freezer (they take about the same time to cook).

Metric	US	Imperial	
175g	1 cup	6oz	plain flour
2·5ml	½ tsp	½ tsp	salt
			good seasoning of black pepper
			pinch of cayenne pepper
125g	1 stick	4oz	butter or margarine
125g	⅔ cup	4oz	finely grated Parmesan cheese
1	1	1	large egg yolk
about 15ml	about 2 tbsp	about 2 tbsp	milk

Grease a baking tray.
Pre-heat the oven to 180°C/350°F/gas mark 4.

Sieve the flour and seasonings together into a bowl, then add the fat roughly cut in lumps. Rub into the flour until the mixture resembles coarse breadcrumbs. Stir in the grated cheese, then mix in the egg yolk and enough milk to bind the pastry together. Knead lightly to eliminate any cracks, then roll out on a lightly floured work surface, until about 3-5mm/⅛-¼ inch thick. Cut into a neat rectangle either 7·5cm/3in or 15cm/6in wide.

Transfer this rectangle to the prepared baking tray and, using a sharp knife, cut into straws 7·5cm/3in long and 6mm/¼ in wide. Separate each straw slightly. Re-roll the pastry scraps to make more straws.

Bake for about 10 minutes, or until cooked through and a golden colour. Remove from the oven and cool on a wire rack. Serve warm, or cool completely and store in an airtight container.

Index